glencoe
teenhealth

building character
+ preventing bullying

Mc
Graw
Hill

Bothell, WA • Chicago, IL • Columbus, OH • New York, NY

Meet the Authors

Mary H. Bronson, Ph.D. recently retired after teaching for 30 years in Texas public schools. Dr. Bronson taught health education in grades K–12 as well as health education methods classes at the graduate and undergraduate levels. As Health Education Specialist for the Dallas School District, Dr. Bronson developed and implemented a district-wide health eduation program. She has been honored as Texas Health Educator of the Year by the Texas Association for Health, Physical Education, Recreation, and Dance and selected Teacher of the Year twice by her colleagues. Dr. Bronson has assisted school districts throughout the country in developing local health education programs. She is also the coauthor of Glencoe Health.

Michael J. Cleary, Ed.D., C.H.E.S. is a professor at Slippery Rock University, where he teaches methods courses and supervises field experiences. Dr. Cleary taught health education at Evanston Township High School in Illinois and later served as the Lead Teacher Specialist at the McMillen Center for Health Education in Fort Wayne, Indiana. Dr. Cleary has published widely on curriculum development and assessment in K–12 and college health education. Dr. Cleary is also coauthor of Glencoe Health.

Betty M. Hubbard, Ed.D., C.H.E.S. has taught science and health education in grades 6–12 as well as undergraduate- and graduate-level courses. She is a professor at the University of Central Arkansas, where in addition to teaching she conducts in-service training for health education teachers in school districts throughout Arkansas. In 1991, Dr. Hubbard received the university's teaching excellence award. Her publications, grants, and presentations focus on research-based, comprehensive health instruction. Dr. Hubbard is a fellow of the American Association for Health Education and serves as the contributing editor of the Teaching Ideas feature of the American Journal of Health Education.

Contributing Author

Dinah Zike, M.Ed. is an international curriculum consultant and inventor who has designed and developed educational products and three-dimensional, interactive graphic organizers for more than 35 years. As president and founder of Dinah-Might Adventures, L.P., Dinah is author of more than 100 award-winning educational publications. Dinah has a B.S. and an M.S. in educational curriculum and instruction from Texas A&M University. Dinah Zike's Foldables® are an exclusive feature of McGraw-Hill.

MHEonline.com

Send all inquiries to:
McGraw-Hill Education
STEM Learning Solutions Center
8787 Orion Place
Columbus, OH 43240

ISBN: 978-0-07-664055-3
MHID: 0-07-664055-8

Printed in the United States of America.

9 10 11 12 LMN 23 22 21 20

STEM McGraw-Hill is committed to providing instructional materials in Science, Technology, Engineering, and Mathematics (STEM) that give all students a solid foundation, one that prepares them for college and careers in the 21st century.

Reviewers

Professional Reviewers

Amy Eyler, Ph.D., CHES
Washington University in St. Louis
St. Louis, Missouri

Shonali Saha, M.D.
Johns Hopkins School of Medicine
Baltimore, Maryland

Roberta Duyff
Duyff & Associates
St. Louis, MO

Teacher Reviewers

Lou Ann Donlan
Altoona Area School District
Altoona, PA

Steve Federman
Loveland Intermediate School
Loveland, Ohio

Rick R. Gough
Ashland Middle School
Ashland, Ohio

Jacob Graham
Oblock Junior High
Plum, Pennsylvania

William T. Gunther
Clarkston Community Schools
Clarkston, MI

Ellie Hancock
Somerset Area School District
Somerset, PA

Diane Hursky
Independence Middle School
Bethel Park, PA

Veronique Javier
Thomas Cardoza Middle School
Jackson, Mississippi

Patricia A. Landon
Patrick F. Healy Middle School
East Orange, NJ

Elizabeth Potash
Council Rock High School South
Holland, PA

The Path to Good Health

Your health book has many features that will aid you in your learning. Some of these features are listed below. You can use the map at the right to help you find these and other special features in the book.

* The **Big Idea** can be found at the start of each lesson.

* Your **Foldables®** help you organize your notes.

* The **Quick Write** at the start of each lesson will help you think about the topic and give you an opportunity to write about it in your journal.

* The **Bilingual Glossary** contains vocabulary terms and definitions in Spanish and English.

* **Health Skills Activities** help you learn more about each of the 10 health skills.

* **Infographs** provide a colorful, visual way to learn about current health news and trends.

* The **Fitness Zone** provides an online fitness resource that includes podcasts, videos, activity cards, and more!

* **Hands-On Health Activities** give you the opportunity to complete hands-on projects.

* **Videos** encourage you to explore real life health topics.

* **Audio** directs you to online audio chapter summaries.

* **Web Quest** activities challenge you to relate lesson concepts to current health news and research.

* **Review** your understanding of health concepts with lesson reviews and quizzes.

What's the word on the street? The **glossary** lists vocabulary terms in English and Spanish.

Quick! Write about your good health habits using a **Quick Write** activity.

Think big! Start your journey with a **Big Idea** and increase your pace with **Foldables®**.

Sharpen your skills with **Health Skills Activities**.

Got a nose for news? Check out each chapter's **infographs** for health news and trends.

Get into the zone –the **Fitness Zone!** Listen to podcasts, watch videos, and more.

Show what you know by completing a **Hands-On Health Activity**.

Stop! Look and Listen! Watch a Health eSpotlight **video** and explore real life health topics. Listen to the **audio** summaries to review the chapter.

Go on a quest. Take a **Web Quest** to learn more about health news and research.

Finish strong! **Review** your understanding of health concepts with lesson reviews and quizzes.

Contents

FLIP 4 FITNESS

F4F-1 through F4F-9
Flip your book over to see a special section on fitness.

chapter

1 Building Character

chapter

2

Bullying and Cyberbullying

Your Total Health

WHAT IS HEALTH?

Do you know someone you would describe as "healthy"? What kinds of traits do they have? Maybe they are involved in sports. Maybe they just "look" healthy. Looking fit and feeling well are important, but there is more to having good health. Good health also includes getting along well with others and feeling good about yourself.

Your **physical**, **emotional**, and **social** *health* are all **related** and make up your *total* **health.**

Health, the *combination of physical, mental/emotional, and social well-being,* may look like the sides of a triangle. You need all three sides to make the triangle. Each side supports the other two sides. Your physical health, mental/emotional health, and social health are all related and make up your total health.

Physical Health

Physical health is one side of the health triangle. Engaging in physical activity every day will help to build and maintain your physical health. Some of the ways you can improve your physical health include the following:

* **EATING HEALTHY FOODS** Choose nutritious meals and snacks.

* **VISITING THE DOCTOR REGULARLY** Get regular checkups from a doctor and a dentist.

* **CARING FOR PERSONAL HYGIENE** Shower or bathe each day. Brush and floss your teeth at least twice every day.

* **WEARING PROTECTIVE GEAR** When playing sports, using protective gear and following safety rules will help you avoid injuries.

* **GET ENOUGH SLEEP** Most teens need about nine hours of sleep every night.

You can also have good physical health by avoiding harmful behaviors, such as using alcohol, tobacco, and other drugs. The use of tobacco has been linked to many diseases, such as heart disease and cancer.

Mental/Emotional Health

Another side of the health triangle is your mental/emotional health. How do you handle your feelings, thoughts, and emotions each day? You can improve your mental/emotional health by talking and thinking about yourself in a healthful way. Share your thoughts and feelings with your family, a trusted adult, or with a friend.

If you are mentally and emotionally healthy, you can face challenges in a positive way. Be patient with yourself when you try to learn new subjects or new skills. Remember that everybody makes mistakes—including you! Next time you can do better.

Taking action to reach your goals is another way to develop good mental/emotional health. This can help you focus your energy and give you a sense of accomplishment. Make healthful choices, keep your promises, and take responsibility for what you do, and you will feel good about yourself and your life.

Social Health

A third side of the health triangle is your social health. Social health means how you relate to people at home, at school, and everywhere in your world. Strong friendships and family relationships are signs of good social health.

Do you get along well with your friends, classmates, and teachers? Do you spend time with your family? You can develop skills for having good relationships. Good social health includes supporting the people you care about. It also includes communicating with, respecting, and valuing people. Sometimes you may disagree with others. You can disagree and express your thoughts, but be thoughtful and choose your words carefully.

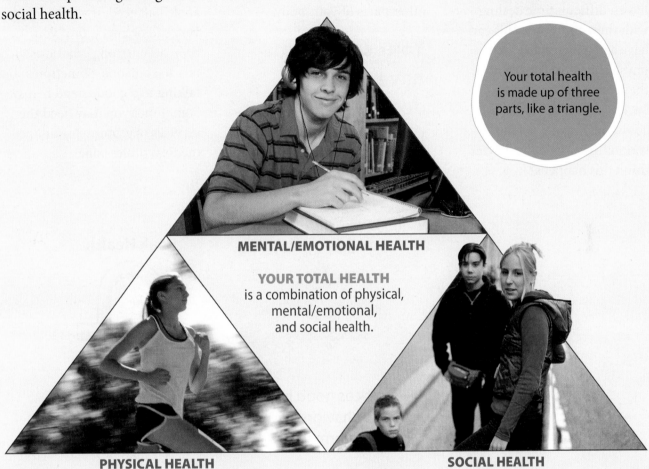

MENTAL/EMOTIONAL HEALTH

YOUR TOTAL HEALTH is a combination of physical, mental/emotional, and social health.

PHYSICAL HEALTH

SOCIAL HEALTH

Your total health is made up of three parts, like a triangle.

ACHIEVING WELLNESS

What is the difference between health and wellness? **Wellness** is *a state of well-being or balanced health over a long period of time.* Your health changes from day to day. One day you may feel tired if you did not get enough sleep. Maybe you worked very hard at sports practice. The next day, you might feel well rested and full of energy because you rested. Your emotions also change. You might feel sad one day but happy the next day.

Your overall health is like a snapshot of your physical, mental/emotional, and social health. Your wellness takes a longer view. Being healthy means balancing the three sides of your health triangle over weeks or months. Wellness is sometimes represented by a continuum, or scale, that gives a picture of your health at a certain time. It may also tell you how well you are taking care of yourself.

The Mind-Body Connection

Your emotions have a lot to do with your physical health. Think about an event in your own life that made you feel sad. How did you deal with this emotion? Sometimes people have a difficult time dealing with their emotions. This can have a negative effect on their physical health. For example, they might get headaches, backaches, upset stomachs, colds, the flu, or even more serious diseases. Why do you think this happens?

Your mind and body connect through your nervous system. This system includes thousands of miles of nerves. The nerves link your brain to your body. Upsetting thoughts and feelings sometimes affect the signals from your brain to other parts of your body.

Your **emotions** have *a lot* to do with *your* **physical health.**

The <u>mind-body connection</u> describes *how your emotions affect your physical and overall health and how your overall health affects your emotions.* This connection shows again how important it is to keep the three sides of the health triangle balanced. If you become very sad or angry, or if you have other strong emotions, talk to someone. Sometimes talking to a good friend helps. Sometimes you may need the services of a counselor or a medical professional.

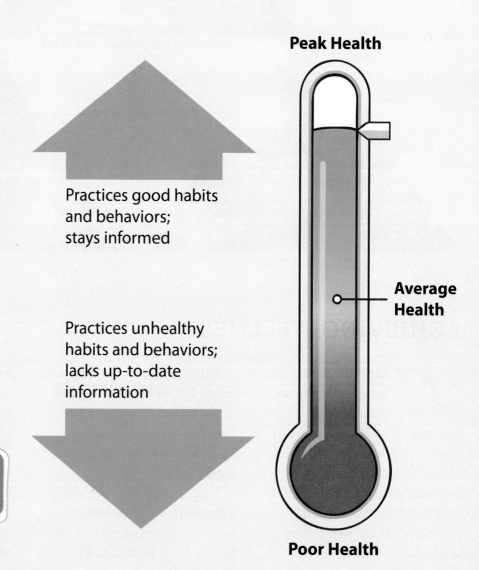

Practices good habits and behaviors; stays informed

Practices unhealthy habits and behaviors; lacks up-to-date information

The Wellness Scale identifies how healthy you are at a given point in time.

Peak Health

Average Health

Poor Health

x

Health Influences *and* Risk Factors

WHAT INFLUENCES YOUR HEALTH?

What are your favorite foods or activities? Your answers reflect your personal tastes, or likes and dislikes. Your health is influenced by your personal tastes and by many other factors such as:

- heredity
- environment
- family and friends
- culture
- media
- attitudes
- behavior

Heredity

You can control some of these factors, but not all of them. For example, you cannot control the natural color of your hair or eyes. **Heredity** (huh•RED•i•tee) is *the passing of traits from parents to their biological children.* Heredity determines the color of your eyes and hair, and other physical traits, or parts of your appearance. Genes are the basic units of heredity. They are made from chemicals called DNA, and they create the pattern for your physical traits. You inherited, or received, half of your DNA from your mother and half from your father.

Environment

Think about where you live. Do you live in a city, a suburb, a small town, or in a rural area? Where you live is the physical part of your **environment** (en•VY•ruhn•mehnt), or *all the living and nonliving things around you.*

Environment is another factor that affects your personal health. Your physical environment includes the home you live in, the school you attend, and the air and water around you.

Your *social environment* includes the people in your life. They can be friends, classmates, and neighbors. Your friends and **peers,** or *people close to you in age who are a lot like you,* may influence your choices.

You may feel pressure to think and act like them. Peer pressure can also influence health choices. The influence can be positive or negative. Helping a friend with homework, volunteering with a friend, or simply listening to a friend are examples of positive peer influence. A friend who wants you to drink alcohol, for example, is a negative influence. Recreation is also a part of your social environment. Playing games and enjoying physical activities with others can have a positive effect on your health.

Traits such as eye and hair color are inherited from parents.

©Jenny Elia Pfeiffer/Corbis

Culture

Your family is one of the biggest influences on your life. It shapes your cultural background, or *the beliefs, customs, and traditions of a specific group of people.* You learned that your family influences your health. In addition to your family, your culture, or *the collected beliefs, customs, and behaviors of a group,* also affects your health. Your family and their culture may influence the foods you eat as well as the activities and special events you celebrate with special foods. Some families fast (do not eat food) during religious events. Ahmed's family observes the holiday of Ramadan.

During this holiday, members of his family fast until sundown. Your family might also celebrate traditions that include dances, foods, ceremonies, songs, and games. Your culture can also affect your health. Knowing how your lifestyle and family history relate to health problems can help you stay well.

Media

What do television, radio, movies, magazines, newspapers, books, billboards, and the Internet have in common? They are all forms of media, or *various methods for communicating information.* The media is another factor that affects your personal health.

The media provide powerful sources of information and influence.

You may learn helpful new facts about health on the Internet or television. You might also see a commercial for the latest video game or athletic shoes. The goal of commercials on television or the Internet, as well as advertisements in print, is to make you want to buy a product. The product may be good or bad for your health. You can make wise health choices by learning to evaluate, or *determine the quality* of everything you see, hear, or read.

The celebration of Kwanzaa is a tradition in many African American families.

YOUR BEHAVIOR AND YOUR HEALTH

Do you protect your skin from the sun? Do you get enough sleep so that you are not tired during the day? Do you eat healthful foods? Do you listen to a friend who needs to talk about a problem? Your answers to these questions reflect your personal lifestyle factors, or *the behaviors and habits that help determine a person's level of health.* Positive lifestyle factors promote good health. Negative lifestyle factors promote poor health.

Positive lifestyle factors promote **good** health.

Your attitude, or your *feelings and beliefs,* toward your personal lifestyle factors plays an important role in your health. You will also have greater success in managing your health if you keep a positive attitude. Teens who have a positive attitude about their health are more likely to practice good health habits and take responsibility for their health.

Risk Behaviors

"Dangerous intersection. Proceed with caution." "Don't walk." "No lifeguard on duty." You have probably seen these signs or similar signs. They are posted to warn you about possible risks or dangers and to keep you safe.

Eating well-balanced meals, starting with a good breakfast.

Getting at least 60 minutes of physical activity daily.

Sleeping at least eight hours every night.

Doing your best in school and other activities.

Avoiding tobacco, alcohol, and other drugs.

Following safety rules and wearing protective gear.

Relating well to family, friends, and classmates.

Lifestyle factors affect your personal health.

Risk, or *the chance that something harmful may happen to your health and wellness,* is part of everyday life. Some risks are easy to identify. Everyday tasks such as preparing food with a knife or crossing a busy street both carry some risk. Other risks are more hidden. Some foods you like might be high in fat.

You cannot avoid every kind of risk. However, the risks you can avoid often involve risk behavior. A risk behavior is an action or behavior that might cause injury or harm to you or others. Playing a sport can be risky, but if you wear protective gear, you may avoid injury. Wear a helmet when you ride a bike to avoid the risk of a head injury if you fall. Smoking cigarettes is another risk behavior that you can avoid. Riding in a car without a safety belt is a risk behavior you can avoid by buckling up. Another risk behavior is having a lifestyle with little physical activity, such as sitting in front of the TV or a computer instead of being active. You can avoid many kinds of risk by taking responsibility for your personal health behaviors and avoiding risk.

RISKS AND CONSEQUENCES

All risk behaviors have consequences. Some consequences are minor or short-term. You might eat a sweet snack just before dinner so that you lose your appetite for a healthy meal. Other risk behaviors may have serious or life-threatening consequences. These are long-term consequences.

Experimenting with alcohol, tobacco, or other drugs has long-term consequences that can seriously damage your health. They can affect all three sides of your health triangle. They can lead to dangerous addictions, which are physical and mental dependencies.

These substances can confuse the user's judgment and can increase the risks he or she takes. Using these substances may also lead to problems with family and friends, and problems at school.

Risks that affect your health are more complicated when they are **cumulative risks** (KYOO•myuh•luh•tiv), which occur *when one risk factor adds to another to increase danger.* For example, making unhealthy food choices is one risk. Not getting regular physical activity is another risk. Add these two risks together over time, and you raise your risk of developing diseases such as heart disease and cancer.

Many choices you make affect your health. Knowing the consequences of your choices and behaviors can help you take responsibility for your health.

Reducing Risks

Practicing prevention, *taking steps to avoid something,* is the best way to deal with risks. For example, wear a helmet when you ride a bike to help prevent head injury. Slow down when walking or running on wet or icy pavement to help prevent a fall. Prevention also means watching out for possible dangers. When you know dangers are ahead, you can avoid them and prevent accidents.

Physical injury can be a consequence of risk behaviors.

EReproductions Ltd/Blend Images LLC

xiv

STAYING INFORMED You can take responsibility for your health by staying informed. Learn about developments in health to maintain your own health. Getting a physical exam at least once a year by a doctor is another way to stay informed about your health.

CHOOSING ABSTINENCE

If you practice abstinence from risk behaviors, you care for your own health and others' health by preventing illness and injury. Abstinence is *the conscious, active choice not to participate in high-risk behaviors.* By choosing not to use tobacco, you may avoid getting lung cancer. By staying away from alcohol, illegal drugs, and sexual activity, you avoid the negative consequences of these risk behaviors.

Abstinence is good for all sides of your health triangle. It promotes your physical health by helping you avoid injury and illness. It protects your mental/emotional health by giving you peace of mind. It also benefits your relationships with family members, peers, and friends. Practicing abstinence shows you are taking responsibility for your personal health behaviors and that you respect yourself and others. You can feel good about making positive health choices, which will strengthen your mental/emotional health as well as your social health.

☑ Plan ahead.

☑ Think about consequences.

☑ Resist negative pressure from others.

☑ Stay away from risk takers.

☑ Pay attention to what you are doing.

☑ Know your limits.

☑ Be aware of dangers.

Reducing risk behaviors will help maintain your overall health.

Getting regular checkups is one form of prevention.

Building Health Skills

SKILLS FOR A HEALTHY LIFE

Health skills are *skills that help you become and stay healthy.* Health skills can help you improve your physical, mental/emotional, and social health. Just as you learn math, reading, sports, and other kinds of skills, you can learn skills for taking care of your health now and for your entire life.

These ten skills affect your physical, mental/emotional, and social health and can benefit you throughout your life.

Health Skills	What It Means to You
Accessing Information	You know how to find valid and reliable health information and health-promoting products and services.
Practicing Healthful Behaviors	You take action to reduce risks and protect yourself against illness and injury.
Stress Management	You find healthy ways to reduce and manage stress in your life.
Analyzing Influences	You recognize the many factors that influence your health, including culture, media, and technology.
Communication Skills	You express your ideas and feelings and listen when others express theirs.
Refusal Skills	You can say no to risky behaviors.
Conflict-Resolution Skills	You can work out problems with others in healthful ways.
Decision Making	You think through problems and find healthy solutions.
Goal Setting	You plan for the future and work to make your plans come true.
Advocacy	You take a stand for the common good and make a difference in your home, school, and community.

SELF-MANAGEMENT SKILLS

When you were younger, your parents and other adults decided what was best for your health. Now that you are older, you make many of these decisions for yourself. You take care of your personal health. You are developing your self-management skills. Two key self-management skills are practicing healthful behaviors and managing stress. When you eat healthy foods and get enough sleep, you are taking actions that promote good health. Stress management is learning to cope with challenges that put a strain on you mentally or emotionally.

Practicing Healthful Behaviors

Your behaviors affect your physical, mental/emotional, and social health. You will see benefits quickly when you practice healthful behaviors. If you exercise regularly, your heart and muscles grow stronger. When you eat healthful foods and drink plenty of water, your body works well.

Getting a good night's sleep will help you wake up with more energy. Respecting and caring for others will help you develop healthy relationships. Managing your feelings in positive ways will help you avoid actions you may regret later.

Staying **positive** is a **good health** *habit.*

Practicing healthful behaviors can help prevent injury, illness, and other health problems. When you practice healthful actions, you can help your total health. Your total health means your physical, mental/emotional, and social health. This means you take care of yourself and do not take risks. It means you learn health-promoting habits. When you eat well-balanced meals and

healthful snacks and get regular physical checkups you are practicing good health habits. Staying positive is another good health habit.

Managing Stress

Learning ways to deal with stress, *the body's response to real or imagined dangers or other life events,* is an important self-management skill. Stress management can help you learn ways to deal with stress. Stress management means identifying sources of stress. It also means you learn how to handle stress in ways that support good health. Relaxation is a good way to deal with stress. Exercise is another way to positively deal with stress.

Studying for a test can cause stress.

Making Decisions *and* Setting Goals

The path to good health begins with making good decisions. You may make more of your own decisions now. Some of those decisions might be deciding which clothes to buy or which classes to take.

As you grow older, you gain more freedom, but with it comes more responsibility. You will need to understand the short-term and long-term consequences of decisions.

Another responsibility is goal setting. You also need to plan how to reach those goals.

When you learn how to set realistic goals, you take a step toward health and well-being. Learning to make decisions and to set goals will help give you purpose and direction in your life.

ACCESSING INFORMATION

Knowing how to get **reliable,** or *trust-worthy and dependable,* health information is an important skill. Where can you find all this information? A main source is from adults you can trust. Community resources give you other ways to get information. These include the library and government health agencies. Organizations such as the American Red Cross can also provide good information.

Reliable Sources

You can find facts about health and health-enhancing products or services through media sources such as television, radio, and the Internet. TV and radio interviews with health professionals can give you information about current scientific studies related to health.

Web sites that end in .gov and .edu are often the most reliable sites. These sites are maintained by government organizations and educational institutions.

Getting health information is important, but so is analyzing whether that health information is valid, or reliable. Carefully review web sites ending in .org.

Many of these sites are maintained by organizations, such as the American Cancer Society or American Diabetes Association. However, some sites ending in .org may not be legitimate.

The Internet can be a good source of health information.

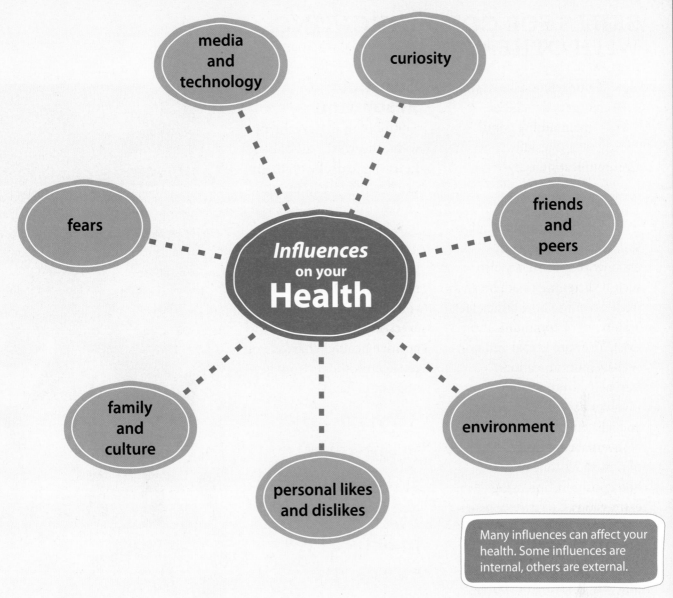

media
and
technology

curiosity

fears

Influences
on your
Health

friends
and
peers

family
and
culture

environment

personal likes
and dislikes

Many influences can affect your health. Some influences are internal, others are external.

Analyzing Influences

Learning how to analyze health information, products, and services will help you act in ways that protect your health. The first step in analyzing an influence is to identify its source. A TV commercial may tell you a certain food has health benefits.

Your **decisions** have to do with your *own* **values** and **beliefs.**

Ask yourself who is the source of the information. Next, think about the motive, or reason, for the influence. Does the advertiser really take your well-being into consideration? Does the ad make you curious about the product?

Does it try to scare you into buying the product? Analyzing influences involves recognizing factors that affect or influence your health.

Your decisions also have to do with your own values and beliefs. The opinions of your friends and family members affect your decisions. Your culture and messages from the media also affect your decisions.

SKILLS FOR COMMUNICATING WITH OTHERS

Your relationships with others depend on maintaining good communication skills. Communication is *the exchange of information through the use of words or actions.* Good communication skills include telling others how you feel. They also include listening to others and understanding how others feel. Two types of communication exist. They are verbal and nonverbal communication. Verbal communication involves a speaker or writer, and a listener or reader. Nonverbal communication includes tone of voice, body position, and using expressions.

Refusal Skills

An important communication skill is saying no. It may be something that is wrong. It may be something that you are not comfortable doing. You may worry what will happen if you don't go along with the group. Will your friends still like you? Will you still be a part of the group? It is at these times that refusal skills, or *strategies that help you say no effectively,* can help. Using refusal skills can sometimes be challenging, but they can help you stay true to yourself and to your beliefs. Also, other people will have respect for you for being honest.

Conflict Resolution

Conflicts, or disagreements with others, are part of life. Learning to deal with them in a healthy way is important. Conflict resolution is *a life skill that involves solving a disagreement in a way that satisfies both sides.* Conflict-resolution skills can help you find a way to satisfy everyone. Also, by using this positive health behavior, you can keep conflicts from getting out of hand.

Conflict resolution skills can help you find a way to *satisfy* everyone.

Advocacy

People with advocacy skills *take action in support of a cause.* They work to bring about a change by speaking out for something like health and wellness. When you speak out for health, you encourage other people to live healthy lives. Advocacy also means keeping others informed.

Using refusal skills effectively can help you avoid potentially dangerous situation.

Image Source/Getty Images

Making Decisions *and* Setting Goals

DECISIONS AND YOUR HEALTH

As you grow up, you usually gain more privileges. Along with privileges comes responsibility. You will make more of your own decisions. The choices and decisions you make can affect each part of your health triangle.

As you get older, you will learn to make more important decisions. You will need to understand the short-term and long-term consequences of the decisions you make.

> You can learn the skill of making good decisions.

Some decisions may help you avoid harmful behaviors. These questions can help you understand some of the consequences of health-related decisions.

- How will this decision affect my health?
- Will it affect the health of others? If so, how?
- Is the behavior I might choose harmful or illegal?
- How will my family feel about my decision?
- Does this decision fit with my values?
- How will this decision affect my goals?

THE DECISION-MAKING PROCESS

You make decisions every day. Some decisions are easy to make. Other decisions are more difficult. Understanding the process of **decision making,** or *the process of making a choice or solving a problem,* will help you make the best possible decisions. The decision-making process can be broken down into six steps. You can apply these six steps to any decision you need to make.

Step 1: State the Situation
Identify the situation as you understand it. When you understand the situation and your choices you can make a sound decision. Ask yourself: What choice do you need to make? What are the facts? Who else is involved?

Step 2: List the Options
When you feel like you understand your situation, think of your options. List all of the possibilities you can think of. Be sure to include only those options that are safe. It is also important to ask an adult you trust for advice when making an important decision.

Step 3: Weigh the Possible Outcomes

After listing your options, you need to evaluate the consequences of each option. The word H.E.L.P. can be used to work through this step of the decision-making process.

- **H** (Healthful) What health risks will this option present to me and to others?
- **E** (Ethical) Does this choice reflect what my family and I believe to be ethical, or right? Does this choice show respect for me and others?
- **L** (Legal) Will I be breaking the law? Is this legal for someone my age?
- **P** (Parent Approval) Would my parents approve of this choice?

Step 4: Consider Your Values

Always consider your values or the beliefs that guide the way you live. Your values reflect what is important to you and what you have learned is right and wrong. Honesty, respect, consideration, and good health are values.

Step 5: Make a Decision and Act

You've weighed your options. You've considered the risks and consequences. Now you're ready for action. Choose the option that seems best for you. Remember that this step is not complete until you take action.

Step 6: Evaluate the Decision

Evaluating the results can help you make better decisions in the future. To evaluate the results, ask yourself: Was the outcome positive or negative? Were there any unexpected outcomes? Was there anything you could have done differently? How did your decision affect others? Do you think you made the right decision? What have you learned from the experience? If the outcome was not what you expected, try again.

Understanding the decision-making process will help you make sound decisions.

Step 1
State the situation.

Step 2
List the options.

Step 3
Weigh the possible outcomes.

Step 4
Consider your values.

Step 5
Make a decision and act.

Step 6
Evaluate the decision.

SETTING REALISTIC GOALS

When you think about your future, what do you see? Do you see someone who has graduated from college and has a good job? Are there things you want to achieve? Answering these questions can give you an idea of your goals in life. A goal is something you want to accomplish.

Goal setting is *the process of working toward something you want to accomplish.* When you have learned to set realistic goals, they can help you focus on what you want to accomplish in life. Realistic goals are goals you can reach.

Setting goals can benefit your health. Many goals can help to improve your overall health. Think about all you want to accomplish in life. Do you need to set some health-related goals to be able to accomplish those things?

Goals can become milestones and can tell you how far you have come. Reaching goals can be a powerful boost to your self-confidence. Improving your self-confidence can help to strengthen your mental/emotional health.

Types of Goals

There are two basic types of goals—**short-term goals,** *goals that you can achieve in a short length of time,* and **long-term goals,** *goals that you plan to reach over an extended period of time.* As the names imply, short-term goals can be accomplished more quickly than long-term goals.

Reaching *goals* can be a powerful *boost* to your self confidence.

Getting your homework turned in on time might be a short-term goal. Long-term goals are generally accomplished over months or years. Getting a college education might be a long-term goal. Often long-term goals are made up of short-term goals.

Jamie has set a goal to be chosen for the all-star team

Reaching Your Goals

To accomplish your short-term and long-term goals, you need a plan. A goal-setting plan that has a series of steps for you to take can be very effective in helping you accomplish your goals. Following a plan can help you make the best use of your time, energy, and other resources. Here are the steps of a goal-setting plan:

- Step 1: Identify a specific goal and write it down. Write down exactly what your goal is. Be sure the goal is realistic.
- Step 2: List the steps to reach your goal. Breaking big goals into smaller goals can make them easier to accomplish.
- Step 3: Get help and support from others. There are many people in your life who can help you reach your goals. They may be parents, teachers, coaches, or other trusted adults.
- Step 4: Evaluate your progress. Check periodically to see if you are actually progressing toward your goal. You may have to identify and consider how to overcome an obstacle before moving toward your goal.
- Step 5: Celebrate when you reach your goal. Give yourself a reward.

Choosing Health Services

WHAT IS HEALTH CARE?

You will probably at some point need to seek health care services. Health care provides services that promote, maintain, or restore health to individuals or communities. The health care system is all the medical care available to a nation's people, the way they receive the care, and the way the care is paid for. It is through the health care system that people receive medical services.

← Emergency

HEALTH CARE PROVIDERS

Many different professionals can help you with your health care. You may be most familiar with your own doctor who is your primary care provider: a health care professional who provides checkups and general care. Nurse practitioners and physician's assistants can also provide primary care.

In addition to doctors, nurse practitioners, and physician's assistants, many other health care professionals provide care. Nurses, pharmacists, health educators, counselors, mental health specialists, dentists, and nutritionists are all health care providers.

Preventive Care

Getting regular checkups is one way to prevent health problems and maintain wellness. During a checkup, your health care provider will check you carefully. She or he will check your heart and lungs and vision and hearing. You may also receive any immunizations you need. During your visit, your doctor may talk to you about healthful eating, exercise, avoiding alcohol, tobacco, and drugs, and other types of preventive care, or steps taken to keep disease or injury from happening or getting worse.

Specialists

Sometimes your primary care provider is not able to help you. In that case, he or she will refer you to a specialist, or health care professional trained to treat a special category of patients or specific health problems. Some specialists treat specific types of people. Other specialists treat specific conditions or body systems.

Specialist	Specialty
Allergist	Asthma, hay fever, other allergies
Cardiologist	Heart problems
Dermatologist	Skin conditions and diseases
Oncologist	Cancer
Ophthalmologist	Eye diseases
Orthodontist	Tooth and jaw irregularities
Orthopedist	Broken bones and similar problems
Otolaryngologist	Ear, nose, and throat
Pediatrician	Infants, children, and teens

Different specialists treat different conditions.

HEALTH CARE SETTINGS

Years ago, people were very limited as to where they could go for health care. In more recent years, new types of health care delivery settings have been developed. People now can go to their doctors' offices, hospitals, surgery centers, hospices, and assisted living communities.

Doctors' Offices

Doctors' offices are probably the most common setting for receiving health care. Your doctor, nurse practitioner, or physician's assistant has medical equipment to help them diagnose illnesses and to give checkups. Most of your medical needs can be met at your doctor's office.

Hospitals

If your medical needs cannot be met at your doctor's office, you may need to go to the hospital. Hospitals have much more medical equipment for diagnosing and treating illnesses. They have rooms for doing surgery and for emergency medicine. They have rooms for patients to stay overnight, if necessary. Hospitals have staff on duty around the clock every day of the year.

Surgery Centers

Your doctor may recommend that you go to a surgery center rather than a hospital. Surgery centers are facilities that offer outpatient surgical care. This means that the patients do not stay overnight. They go home the same day they have the surgery. Serious surgeries cannot be done in a surgery center. They would be done in a hospital where the patient can stay and recover. For general outpatient care, many people go to clinics.

Clinics

Clinics are similar to doctors' offices and often have primary care physicians and specialists on staff. If you go to a clinic, you might not see the same doctor each time you go. You might see whoever is on duty that day. This might make it more difficult for the doctor to get to know you and your health issues. However, for people who do not need to go to the doctor often, a clinic might be a good fit.

Hospice Care

Hospice care provides a place where terminally ill patients can live out the remainder of their lives. Terminally ill patients will not recover from their illness. Hospice workers are specially trained and are experts in pain management. They are also trained and skilled at giving emotional support to the family and the patient. Many terminally ill patients receive hospice care in their own homes. Nurses visit the patient in their own home and provide medications for pain. They also spend time with family members, helping them learn to cope during the emotionally difficult time.

Pixtal/AGE Fotostock

Assisted Living Communities

As people get older, they may not be able to take care of themselves as well as they used to. Assisted living communities offer older people an alternative to nursing homes. In nursing homes, all of the resident's needs are taken care of. In assisted living communities, the residents can choose which services they need. They may be unable to drive and need transportation. They may need reminders to take medications. They may need to have food prepared for them. In an assisted living community, the residents are able to live in their own apartments as long as they are able. Medical staff is available when the residents need help.

PAYING FOR HEALTH CARE

Health care costs can be expensive. Many people buy health insurance to help pay for medical costs. Health insurance is a plan in which a person pays a set fee to an insurance company in return for the company's agreement to pay some or all medical expenses when needed. They pay a monthly premium, or fee, to the health insurance company for the policy. There are several different options when choosing health insurance.

Private Health Care Plans

One health insurance option is managed care. Health insurance plans emphasize preventative medicine and work to control the cost and maintain the quality of health care. Using managed care, patients save money when they visit doctors who participate in the managed care plan. There are several different managed care plans such as a health maintenance organization (HMO), a preferred provider organization (PPO), and a point-of-service (POS) plan.

Government Public Health Care Plans

The government currently offers two types of health insurance—Medicaid and Medicare. Medicaid is for people with limited income. Medicare is for people over the age of 65 and for people of any age with certain disabilities.

Following a logical plan can help you achieve many goals.

Building Character

LESSONS

PREMIUM ONLINE RESOURCES

 Audio　　 Videos　　 Bilingual Glossary

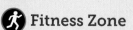 Fitness Zone　　 Web Quest　　 Review

Working together to help others is one way to build character. *Explain how you think volunteering can help build character.*

What *is* Character?

BIG IDEA ▶ Character is the way a person thinks, feels, and acts.

Before You Read

QUICK WRITE Write a short description of a person who has been a positive role model for you.

▶ Video

As You Read

FOLDABLES Study Organizer

Make the Foldable® on page 40 to record the information presented in Lesson 1.

Vocabulary

› character
› integrity
› tolerance
› prejudice
› accountability
› advocacy
› role model

◀)) Audio

🄰🄱🄲 Bilingual Glossary

UNDERSTANDING CHARACTER

MAIN IDEA ▶ A person's character demonstrates his or her values and beliefs.

Do you tell the truth? Do you respect others? These are some signs of good **character,** or *the way a person thinks, feels, and acts.* Good character is an important part of a healthy identity.

Six Traits *of* Good Character

You are a member of many groups, like a family, a sports team, or friends. In order for people to get along, they need to have good character traits, including: trustworthiness, respect, responsibility, fairness, caring, and citizenship.

> *Good character is an important part of a healthy identity.*

TRUSTWORTHINESS If you are honest, loyal, and reliable, you earn people's trust. This is trustworthiness. You show the courage to do the right thing.

For example, a friend may ask you to do something that goes against your values, such as using tobacco. If you say no to remain true to your values, you show integrity. **Integrity** is *being true to your ethical values* and doing what you know is right.

RESPECT You show respect by being considerate of others and accepting their differences. It does not mean that you must agree with everything that another person says or does. With respect you show **tolerance** (TAHL·er·ence), *the ability to accept other people as they are.* You avoid *negative and unjustly formed opinions,* or **prejudice** (PREH·juh·dis), that includes fears formed without having facts or firsthand knowledge. **RESPONSIBILITY** You hold yourself accountable for your choices, decisions, and actions. **Accountability** is *a willingness to answer for your actions and decisions.* You think about consequences before you act.

Design Pics/SW Productions

FAIRNESS You play by the rules, take turns, and share. You listen to others. You do not take advantage of other people or blame them when things don't go the way you expect.

CARING You show that you are kind and considerate of others.

Caring includes showing gratitude and helping others.

CITIZENSHIP You show respect for authority and interest in the world around you, including the health and safety at school and in your community. You can show this respect through

advocacy, *taking action in support of a cause,* and taking a stand to make a difference.

>>> **Reading Check**
IDENTIFY *What are the six traits of good character?*

WHAT SHAPES YOUR CHARACTER?

MAIN IDEA Your life experiences and role models shape your character.

Many influences shape your character. From an early age, you learn values from your family members. As you mature, you make your own choices about what kind of character you will have.

Do you value honesty in others? You may choose to always be honest. Do you see fairness around you? You may choose to be fair. You may learn that you appreciate kindness in others, and choose to be kind. You choose and practice to have good character.

What Influences character?
Many factors can influence a person's character. List other facts that are not shown here.

Life Experiences

Character is shaped by your family and the people around you. If you learned to share and respect your siblings, you learned fairness and respect. As you mature, your teachers, other adults, and friends can shape your character.

Do you *value* honesty in others?

When you find someone you trust, you learn about being trustworthy. At school, you learn to be responsible for your schoolwork, to follow the rules, and to care for others. As you learn about your community, you learn about citizenship.

Role Models

One way to learn about character is to watch and listen to others. You learn to model your actions by examples. A role model is *a person who inspires you to think or act a certain way* and whose behavior serves as a good example. A teacher may be a model of responsibility and fairness. A coach might model trustworthiness and respect. Family members may model caring.

>>> **Reading Check**
EXPLAIN *Who are the first teachers of character?*

Parents or Guardians	Stories	Life Experiences	Examples Set by Others
The earliest influence on your character was likely a parent or guardian. Parents and guardians are our first teachers of character.	Have you heard the expression, that's the moral of the story? Many stories contain a moral. The moral teaches about values or character traits.	You learn from things you do in your life. You may have done something that turned out to be a mistake. Did you learn from that mistake?	Role models inspire us to act or think in a certain way. They set good examples. Who do you look up to for inspiration?

DEVELOPING GOOD CHARACTER

MAIN IDEA Good character means making good choices.

Mia and her older sister, Megan, are in the grocery store shopping for groceries. As they walk down an aisle, Megan looks down on the ground and notices a $20 dollar bill. Megan quickly takes the money to a store manager. The manager thanks Megan and Mia for turning in the money. Mia is proud of her sister for demonstrating responsibility and trustworthiness.

As you watch, listen to, and learn from others, you choose the traits you want to demonstrate your character. You develop character that becomes a way of life and a part of who you are. For example, if you do your family chores, you demonstrate responsibility. If you listen to different points of view, you demonstrate respect. When you help a person in need, you demonstrate caring and kindness.

*Good character is something anyone can **choose**.*

Demonstrating good character is a choice. If you choose to be honest, you will tell the truth and you will not cheat. If you obey the rules and respect authority, you are choosing citizenship. You practice making choices to demonstrate good character. Good character is something anyone can choose. The more you practice the traits you value, the more they become a part of your character.

>>> **Reading Check**

ANALYZE *What are two ways to develop good character?* ■

>>> **After You Read**

1. **VOCABULARY** Define the term *character*. Use it in a sentence.
2. **EXPLAIN** Tell how good character contributes to physical, mental/emotional, and social health.
3. **IDENTIFY** Name two traits that show good character.

>>> **Thinking Critically**

4. **HYPOTHESIZE** Think of an act of citizenship you know about. It can be an act of someone you know, or someone you have read about or seen on TV. Tell how the act demonstrates citizenship. Does the example include any other traits of good character? If so, tell how.

>>> **Applying Health Skills**

5. **ANALYZING INFLUENCES** Name two people you know or know about who could be good role models. Explain how each person demonstrates good character and what you might learn from each person.

⟳ Review

◉ Audio

Working together can build good character. *Explain what traits of good character can show when working together.*

McGraw-Hill Companies, Inc. Digital Light Source/Richard Hutchings, photographer

Trustworthiness *and* Respect

BIG IDEA Good character is built on trustworthiness and respect.

Before You Read

QUICK WRITE Write your own definition of trust. Can you name people in your life who are trustworthy?

▶ Video

As You Read

STUDY ORGANIZER Make the study organizer on page 40 to record the information presented in Lesson 2.

Vocabulary

› loyal

🔊 Audio

🔤 Bilingual Glossary

Developing Good Character

Respect When you are faced with a difficult choice, you want to earn the respect of others, but more importantly, you want to respect yourself. Making healthy decisions shows that you respect yourself and your health. *What are some other ways of showing respect for yourself?*

TRUSTWORTHINESS

MAIN IDEA Trustworthiness is a trait of good character.

Gabriel and Tuan are taking a quiz. Gabriel studied for the quiz and feels prepared. Tuan tries to look at Gabriel's quiz, but Gabriel covers his answers. Gabriel shows trustworthiness and integrity by not allowing Tuan to look at his answers.

If you are honest, other people will trust you. You are trustworthy. If you work on a project with other students, and every day you show up on time with your part of the work complete, your team members will trust you. When you borrow a dollar for lunch and return it the next day, you show trustworthiness. If you tell the truth, do not cheat or steal, you are trustworthy.

Trustworthy people are reliable. They can be relied on to do what is expected and what they say they will do. They show up on time, always tell the truth, and demonstrate that they can be trusted.

If you always bring in your completed homework, your teacher will rely on you to come to class prepared. You demonstrate reliability.

Trustworthy people have integrity. Integrity is the quality of doing what you know is right. Imagine you see a student leave her wallet on the lunch table at school. If you return it immediately, you show integrity. You are doing the right thing.

Integrity is the *quality* of **doing** what you know is *right*.

Being loyal, or *faithful,* makes you trustworthy. Good friends are loyal, or faithful. A loyal friend will not say, or allow others to say, untrue or unkind things about you.

Reading Check

IDENTIFY *Name two characteristics of trustworthiness.*

RESPECT

MAIN IDEA Good character is demonstrated through respect.

Dipali and Lorinda are good friends. Lorinda asks Dipali to come to her house for a party on Friday. When Dipali arrives, she sees that everyone, including Lorinda, is drinking alcohol. Dipali knows she shouldn't be drinking alcohol and decides she needs to leave. Dipali shows that she respects herself and doesn't want to do anything that might risk her health.

Respect means having consideration for the feelings of others. Think about how you want to be treated, and treat others the same way. You show respect with good manners. You show respect by listening to the points of view of others, even when they are different from yours. An important element of respect is tolerance, the ability to accept other people as they are. Our world is made up of people with different cultures and backgrounds.

Learning about people who have different backgrounds can enrich our lives.

Tolerance also prevents prejudice. Prejudice is an opinion or fear formed without facts or full knowledge.

Respect starts with your self. You show self-respect by leading a healthy life. You stay away from high-risk behaviors, such as sexual activity, or tobacco use, alcohol use, and other drug use. You show respect for your body by eating healthful foods, and getting plenty of physical activity and rest.

>>> **Reading Check**

RECALL *Name two ways to show respect for others.* ■

Demonstrations of trustworthiness and respect contribute to good character. *Which of these traits can describe you?*

Trustworthiness	Respect
☐ I always tell the truth.	☐ I am polite to others.
☐ I do what I say I will do.	☐ I listen to other people's opinions.
☐ I do what I know is the right thing.	☐ I accept people who are different from me.
☐ I am loyal to my friends.	☐ I take care of my health.
☐ I never cheat or steal.	☐ I am tolerant of differences in people.

REVIEW

>>> **After You Read**

1. **VOCABULARY** Define the term *integrity*. Use it in a sentence.
2. **IDENTIFY** Name three traits of trustworthiness.
3. **EXPLAIN** Describe how you can demonstrate respect for yourself.

>>> **Thinking Critically**

4. **APPLY** Think about a time you were faced with a decision whether to tell the truth or stay quiet. What did you do?

>>> **Applying Health Skills**

5. **SETTING GUIDELINES** Work with a small group to make a poster that outlines rules for respectful behavior in your school community. Use what you learned in this lesson. When your poster is complete, share it with your class.

⟳ Review

🔊 Audio

Responsibility *and* Fairness

BIG IDEA Acts of responsibility and fairness demonstrate good character.

Before You Read

QUICK WRITE List responsibilities that you believe lie ahead. What responsibilities are you looking forward to?

▶ Video

As You Read

STUDY ORGANIZER Make the study organizer on page 40 to record the information presented in Lesson 3.

Vocabulary

› abstinence

🔊 Audio

🔠 Bilingual Glossary

RESPONSIBILITY

MAIN IDEA Your character shows in your responsibilities.

Yuri has a new puppy. He promises to help take care of the dog. Yuri's friend, Jacob, asks him to go to see a movie after school. Yuri wants to go, but it is his turn to walk the dog. Yuri calls Jacob and asks if they can go to a movie on another day. He accepts responsibility for taking care of his pet.

Showing **responsibility** means doing what you say you will do.

What are some of your responsibilities right now? Do you take responsibility for completing your schoolwork on time? At home, do you make your bed, help with the dishes or the trash? As you get older, you take on more responsibilities. Accepting responsibility includes accountability. When you are accountable for your actions, you do not blame others for your mistakes. You accept the consequences for your actions.

To accept responsibility means to be willing to take on duties and tasks. Showing responsibility means doing what you say you will do. You take credit for things done well and not done so well. When you have a responsibility, you follow through without being asked or reminded.

Taking Responsibility *for* Your Health

As you mature, you take responsibility for your health by making good decisions. You learn that making healthful food choices improves your physical and mental health. You learn to make time for physical activity and to avoid risk behaviors. You learn to practice **abstinence** (AB·stuh·nuhns), which is your *conscious, active choice not to participate in high-risk behaviors,* such as sexual activity, tobacco use, alcohol use, and drug use.

> **>>> Reading Check**
> **EXPLAIN** *What does it means to be responsible?*

Responsibility	Fairness
____ Does chores and tasks without reminders.	____ Treats people equally.
____ Keeps promises.	____ Considers new ideas.
____ Thinks before acting.	____ Shares.
____ Makes good decisions about physical and mental health.	____ Takes turns.
____ Does school work on time.	____ Shows good sportsmanship, win or lose.

These traits describe responsibility and fairness.
List the ways in which you demonstrate responsibility and fairness.

FAIRNESS

MAIN IDEA A person who is fair treats everyone equally and honestly.

Abby and her friend Taylor are judging a school art contest. Abby wants to award the prize to Paul because his painting is very good. Taylor wants to award the prize to her friend Katy. "I know Katy is your friend, but Paul really deserves to win," says Abby. "It's only fair to give it to the person who deserves to win." Abby understands the importance of fairness.

Fairness means treating people **equally** and **honestly**.

Good character is also demonstrated with fairness. Fairness means treating people equally and honestly. A person with fairness is open-minded and patient.

A fair person does not take advantage of another person. Many things that you do, such as taking turns and sharing, demonstrate fairness. Fairness includes being a good sport, win or lose.

Many of your actions show responsibility and fairness. For example, you can show fairness while playing sports. Pretend you are playing football with some friends. While you are running with the ball, you accidentally step out of bounds near the goal line. A person on the other team sees you step out of bounds. He or she says that you did not score. What would you do? If you admit that you step out of bounds, you are displaying fairness.

>>> Reading Check

IDENTIFY *Name two traits of fairness.* ■

REVIEW

>>> After You Read

1. **VOCABULARY** Define the term *responsibility*. Use it in an original sentence.
2. **EXPLAIN** Describe ways a teen can be responsible for his or her physical and mental health.
3. **IDENTIFY** Name two traits of fairness.

>>> Thinking Critically

4. **APPLY** Describe a time you lost a game or competition. What did you do? Describe whether your actions showed fairness.

>>> Applying Health Skills

5. **PRACTICING HEALTHFUL BEHAVIORS** Tell about a time you took responsibility for your physical or mental health by making a good decision.

Review

Audio

Being *a* Good Citizen

BIG IDEA Good character includes caring and citizenship.

Before You Read

QUICK WRITE Write a short paragraph to explain how caring for others can benefit your health.

▶ Video

As You Read

STUDY ORGANIZER Make the study organizer on page 40 to record the information presented in Lesson 4.

Vocabulary

› empathy

🔊 Audio

🔤 Bilingual Glossary

CARING FOR OTHERS

MAIN IDEA Good character shows in acts of caring.

Caring means treating other people with kindness and understanding. You show you care when you help and support others. Caring people show gratitude to others who help them. They show forgiveness to those who have hurt them. We show that we care by listening, offering to help others, and looking at others' points of views.

Sometimes, just listening to a person talk about what is bothering him or her is an important act of caring. You may not be able to help the friend with his or her problem. Taking the time to listen shows that you care.

The Spirit *of* Giving

One quality found in caring people is the spirit of giving. This doesn't mean giving of "things," it means giving of yourself: your time, your attention, your help and support. When you show caring and understanding, you are giving your time and attention. You can also give your time and attention to friends and others in your community.

You can also share your skills and experience. If you like to cook, you can share food with classmates or a local shelter. If you are good at a sport, you can play with younger students to help them improve their skills. If you speak Spanish, you can give your time by tutoring other students at school.

Taking the **time** to **listen** shows that you *care*.

Showing Sympathy *and* Empathy

When you care about others, you are kind to them. You show consideration for their feelings. You can show empathy, *the ability to identify with and share another person's feelings.* If a friend is feeling sad or disappointed, you can show empathy by sharing your friend's feelings.

>>> **Reading Check**

DEFINE *What is empathy?*

CITIZENSHIP

MAIN IDEA Good citizens help make a community a better place.

Every individual is a citizen of a community. A community can be your neighborhood, your school, your city, or your country. The way you conduct yourself as a member of a community is citizenship. Citizenship is a part of good character. Teens who obey the rules and follow the laws are good citizens.

Citizenship means doing what you can to help your community. Good citizens work to protect the environment. They keep the environment clean, and recycle paper, glass, and aluminum.

They take a stand to prevent violence and bullying. Good citizens also volunteer in helping the community and environment. They advocate, or take action to support a cause and to help the community.

Caring and citizenship work together. You are a good citizen because you care about other people, the community, and the environment.

> ### ⟫⟫ Reading Check
>
> **IDENTIFY** *List two ways to demonstrate citizenship.* ■

These teens help to keep their community clean. *How do these teens demonstrate citizenship?*

⟫⟫ After You Read

1. **VOCABULARY** Define the term *citizenship*. Use it in an original sentence.
2. **EXPLAIN** Explain what it means to advocate.
3. **IDENTIFY** Name two ways to show good citizenship.

⟫⟫ Thinking Critically

4. **HYPOTHESIZE** Discuss some ways you can give to your community.

⟫⟫ Applying Health Skills

5. **ACCESSING INFORMATION** Search the Internet for "teen volunteer organizations." Some sites will give you the opportunity to type in your city, your ZIP code, or a special interest. Find one site that interests you and share what you learned on the site with your classmates.

🔄 Review

🔊 Audio

Hero Images/Getty Images

McGraw-Hill Companies, Inc. Ken Karp, photographer

Making a Difference

BIG IDEA Your words and actions show your character.

Before You Read

QUICK WRITE List three ways you show that you care.

▶ Video

As You Read

STUDY ORGANIZER Make the study organizer on page 40 to record the information presented in Lesson 5.

Vocabulary

› constructive criticism
› I-messages
› cliques

🔊 Audio

🔤 Bilingual Glossary

Developing Good Character

Respect Older adults have a lot of wisdom and experience to share. You can show respect for older adults by listening and speaking in a polite manner. *What are some other ways you can show respect to older adults?*

CHARACTER IN ACTION

MAIN IDEA Good character helps you develop and maintain healthy relationships.

Your good character shows in your actions and words. Good character improves your own life, and affects everyone around you. Think about all of your relationships: with your family, your friends and classmates, and your community. When your actions and words show good character, you have many good and strong relationships.

Making a Difference at Home

Family relationships are built on caring, respect, fairness, trust, and responsibility. Your actions and words make a difference at home. You can show your character by treating your family members with care and respect. Show appreciation for the things your family does for you. Help out with chores without being asked. Take responsibility for your own chores or tasks. Be patient and kind to your siblings.

You can keep your **good character** even if you have a *problem*

You can keep your good character even if you have a problem at home. Discuss your problem with respect for others. You may want to offer constructive criticism. Constructive criticism is *using a positive message to make a suggestion.* For example, if your younger brother is having trouble tying his shoe, you might offer to demonstrate. You can also make suggestions using I-messages, which are *messages in which you offer a suggestion from your own point of view.* For example, "I can't understand you when you talk with your mouth full."

Reading Check

LIST *Name two ways to build good character at home.*

Making a Difference at School

Good character can make a difference at school. At school, you have relationships with friends, classmates, teachers, and other adults. Good character means showing positive values.

It also means setting good examples of fairness, trustworthiness, caring, and responsibility. You can build your character by accepting others and showing tolerance toward differences.

People tend to feel comfortable around others like themselves.

This sometimes leads to the formation of **cliques**, *groups of friends who hang out together and act in similar ways* and who have same interests and values. Being a part of a clique can provide a person with a sense of belonging. However, cliques can be negative if they exclude others or show prejudice toward those whose interests are different.

You show your character at school by taking responsibility for your schoolwork, obeying school rules, and treating teachers and students with respect.

Teens show good character to their classmates. *How can you show good character to your classmates?*

>>> **Reading Check**

DESCRIBE *How can cliques be harmful? How can they be helpful?*

Health SKILLS ACTIVITY

Advocacy

Relating to Your *Community*

Building a healthy relationship with the community includes the following skills:

* Respect. Show your respect for your community by taking pride in it. Help keep it clean. Avoid littering or defacing property.

* Tolerance. Demonstrate tolerance by getting to know people in your community who are different from you. When you demonstrate tolerance, you encourage others around you to do the same.

With A Group

Create several posters encouraging teens to show respect for their community. Include posters that discuss intolerance and how it affects the community. Your posters should also encourage teens to demonstrate tolerance to others.

©Creatas/PunchStock

Making *a* Difference *in* **Your Community**

You read about how character shows in citizenship. You can make a difference in your community with your acts of citizenship. You protect your environment when you throw away trash and recycle glass, aluminum and papers. You can also help your community by volunteering your time or skills to others.

Most communities have volunteer programs to help others. Volunteers make and serve food to shelters, collect clothes and books to donate to others, and work to help others in different ways.

Volunteers collect and box goods to send to service men and women. Volunteers tutor and coach children. Volunteers take part in activities, such as bake sales or car washes, to collect money for people in need. When you volunteer your time and skills to help others, you make a difference in your community.

As a volunteer, your acts of citizenship show that you advocate fairness, equality, caring, and giving. You are advocating for a better community and better world. ■

Teens give their time to help the community. *Explain how you think it might feel to provide food to hungry people.*

Image Source/Getty Images

REVIEW

>>> **After You Read**

1. **VOCABULARY** Define the term *constructive criticism*. Use it in an original sentence.
2. **EXPLAIN** Describe how a clique can be harmful.
3. **IDENTIFY** List three places to develop your good character.

>>> **Thinking Critically**

4. **APPLY** Think of a public figure who works to help world situations. Use the Internet to learn about how that person works to advocate for change.

>>> **Applying Health Skills**

5. **ADVOCACY** Imagine that a clique of students is bullying another student at lunch and in the school halls. What steps can you take to advocate against bullying? What traits of good character does it take to advocate against bullying?

 Review

🔊 Audio

Hands-On HEALTH ACTIVITY

Developing Good Character

WHAT YOU WILL NEED
* poster board
* markers or crayons

WHAT YOU WILL DO

1 Your teacher will divide the class into six small groups and assign each group one of the six traits of character: trustworthiness, respect, responsibility, fairness, caring, or citizenship.

2 Brainstorm and list examples of how teens can develop the assigned character trait. For example, if your group was assigned trustworthiness, you might list telling the truth and keeping promises.

3 Create a poster featuring the examples you listed in Step 2. As a group, explain to the class how your examples can help a teen develop good character.

WRAPPING IT UP
After all the groups have presented their posters, discuss these questions as a class: How can teens help other teens develop good character? How can good character affect all sides of the health triangle? Display your posters where your classmates can see them.

Character is formed every day by your thoughts and actions. Developing good character is important to your health. It will help you develop positive relationships and behaviors. A person of good character is trustworthy; treats people with respect; is responsible, fair, and caring; and is a good citizen. In this activity, you will create a poster with examples of how to develop one of the six traits of character.

READING REVIEW

FOLDABLES and Other Study Aids

Take out the Foldable® that you created for Lesson 1 and any study organizers that you created for Lessons 2–5. Find a partner and quiz each other using these study aids.

LESSON 1 What is Character?

BIG IDEA Character is the way a person thinks, feels, and acts.

* Good character is part of a healthy identity.
* A person's character demonstrates his or her values and beliefs.
* Your life experiences and role models shape your character.
* Good character means making good choices.

LESSON 2 Trustworthiness and Respect

BIG IDEA Good character is built on trustworthiness and respect.

* Trustworthiness is a trait of good character.
* Trustworthy people can be relied upon to do what they say they will do.
* Integrity is the quality of doing what you know is right.
* Good character is demonstrated through respect.

LESSON 3 Responsibility and Fairness

BIG IDEA Acts of responsibility and fairness demonstrate good character.

* Your character shows in your responsibilities.
* Accepting responsibility includes accountability.
* Taking responsibility for your health includes making good decisions.
* A fair person treats everyone equally and honestly.

LESSON 4 Being a Good Citizen

BIG IDEA Good character includes caring and citizenship.

* Good character shows in acts of caring.
* Caring involves having the spirit of giving and showing sympathy and empathy.
* Good citizens help to make their community a better place.
* Caring and citizenship go together in helping to build character.

LESSON 5 Making a Difference

BIG IDEA Your words and actions show your character.

* Good character helps you develop and maintain healthy relationships.
* Traits of good character include communication skills, respect, tolerance, and citizenship.
* You can demonstrate good character by working to make a difference at home, at school, and in your community.

 Review

 Web Quest

ASSESSMENT

Reviewing Vocabulary *and* Main Ideas

- › role model
- › tolerance
- › character
- › loyal
- › fairness
- › respect
- › abstinence
- › integrity

» On a sheet of paper, write the numbers 1–8. After each number, write the term from the list that best completes each statement

LESSON 1 What is Character?

1. The way a person thinks, feels, and acts is known as _____.

2. The quality of always doing what you know is right is _____.

3. _____ is the ability to accept other people as they are.

4. A _____ is a person who inspires you to think or act a certain way.

LESSON 2 Trustworthiness and Respect

5. To be _____ means you are faithful.

6. Having consideration for the feelings of others is _____.

LESSON 3 Responsibility and Fairness

7. The conscious, active choice not to participate in high-risk behaviors is _____.

8. _____ means treating people equally and honestly.

» On sheet of paper, write the numbers 9-14. Write *True* or *False* for each statement below. If the statement is false, change the underlined word or phrase to make it true.

LESSON 4 Being a Good Citizen

9. If a friend feels sad or depressed, you can show empathy by sharing your friend's feelings.

10. Abstinence means you support a cause.

11. Citizenship means doing what you can to support your community.

LESSON 5 Making a Difference

12. Destructive criticism is using a positive message to make a suggestion.

13. Messages in which you offer a suggestion from your own point of view are called I-messages.

14. Groups of friends who hang out together and act in similar ways are called cliques.

✓ eAssessment

>> Using complete sentences, answer the following questions on a sheet of paper.

 *Thinking* **Critically**

15. ANALYZE List the six traits of good character. Next to each trait, give an example of how someone might demonstrate the trait.

 *Write* **About It**

16. OPINION Imagine you are writing an article on advocating for a school recycling program. In your article, explain why a school recycling program would benefit the students, teachers, and the community.

Ⓐ Ⓑ Ⓒ Ⓓ STANDARDIZED TEST PRACTICE

Reading
Read the passage below and then answer the questions that follow.

Did you know that one in seven people in the world goes to bed hungry every night? Or that people suffer from diseases that were stamped out in this country long ago? We are citizens of many different communities, such as cities or countries. However, we are all citizens of the world. Unfortunately, not all members of the world community share its resources equally.

One way to help suffering communities is by acting as a health advocate. Tell others about the suffering of other nations. Become and stay informed about world events. The World Health Organization is currently taking action to help people in need. Visit their Web site for further information.

1. Which statement best sums up the main point of the passage?
  A. We all live in many different communities.
  B. The health skill of advocacy can be used to help nations in need.
  C. Other countries are suffering from diseases that we have already overcome.

2. The passage notes that "not all members of this global community share its resources equally." Of the following quotes, which is *not* a detail that supports that comment?
  A. "Did you know that one in seven people in the world goes to bed hungry every night?"
  B. "Or that people suffer from diseases that were stamped out in this country long ago?"
  C. "Become and stay informed about world events."

BUILDING CHARACTER

Character is how a person thinks, feels, and acts. Someone with good character has the following traits:

Trustworthiness
Responsibility
Respect
Fairness
Citizenship
Caring

WHAT DO THEY MEAN?

TRUSTWORTHINESS
You are honest, loyal and do what you say you are going to do.

RESPECT
You are considerate of others and accept their differences.

RESPONSIBILITY
You hold yourself accountable for your choices, decisions, and actions.

FAIRNESS
You play by the rules, take turns, and share.

CARING
You show that you are kind and considerate of others.

CITIZENSHIP
You show respect for authority and interest in the world around you.

HOW IS CHARACTER DEVELOPED?

Life experiences

Your family, friends, teachers, and others in your community can shape your character.

Role models

A UCLA School of Public Health study asked 750 teens if they had a role model. Fifty-six percent said they did. Girls most often named a parent or relative as a role model, while boys named a sports star or other public figure.

PUTTING IT INTO ACTION

Your good character shows in your actions and words.

AT HOME

Treat parents and family members with care and respect.

Show appreciation.

Help with chores.

Be patient and kind to siblings.

AT SCHOOL

Take responsibility for your schoolwork.

Obey school rules.

Respect teachers and students.

Take a stand against violence and bullying.

IN YOUR COMMUNITY

Pick up trash and throw away into garbage cans.

Recycle bottles, cans, and paper.

Volunteer your time and talents.

THE BATTLE AGAINST BULLYING

Bullying and cyberbullying are both dangerous and damaging forms of teasing, taunting, intimidation, or harassment.

WHY DOES BULLYING HAPPEN?

BULLIES

- To fit in with a group
- To feel superior
- To avoid being bullied themselves
- Lack of tolerance for those who are different
- Lack of parental supervision

BULLIED

- Being overweight/underweight, being uninterested in sports, wearing different clothing, being new to a school
- Weak or unable to defend themselves
- Depressed, anxious, or insecure with low self-esteem
- Less popular than others and having few friends
- Unable to get along well with others

Cyberbullying

Cyberbullying uses electronic means, like text messages and the Internet.

INSTANT MESSAGES

SOCIAL MEDIA SITES

WEBSITES

ONLINE GAMING SITES

E-MAILS

TEXT MESSAGES

HOW TO PREVENT AND STOP BULLYING
On-the-spot strategies

No one deserves to be bullied. If you are a target, here are some ways to prevent bullying or stop it when it occurs:

TELL THE BULLY TO STOP.

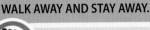

TRY HUMOR.

WALK AWAY AND STAY AWAY.

AVOID PHYSICAL VIOLENCE.

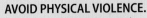

FIND AN ADULT.

CYBERBULLYING

3:20 pm

- Avoid including personal information about yourself.
- Don't post anything online that you wouldn't want others to see.
- Don't forward bullying messages you receive about others.
- Block the person who is cyberbullying.

Bullying + Cyberbullying

LESSONS

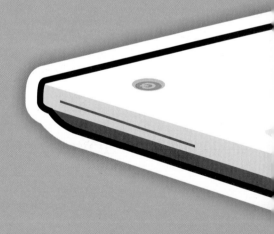

PREMIUM ONLINE RESOURCES

 Audio

 Videos

 Bilingual Glossary

 Fitness Zone

 Web Quest

 Review

People who are bullied can be hurt physically and emotionally. *List two forms of bullying.*

Bullying *and* Harassment

BIG IDEA ▷ Anyone can experience bullying and harassment, but there are effective ways to stop both.

Before You Read

QUICK WRITE Write about three factors you think are responsible for bullying. Share one factor with the class.

▶ Video

As You Read

 Study Organizer

Make the Foldable® on page 41 to record the information presented in Lesson 1.

Vocabulary

› bullying
› labeling
› intimidation
› harassment
› sexual harassment

🔊 Audio

🔠 Bilingual Glossary

WHAT IS BULLYING?

MAIN IDEA ▷ Most students have been bullied at one time or another.

Josh was waiting in the school lunch line. Suddenly, he felt someone shove him. Josh then heard Rick and his friends laughing "Move out of the way, loser," as the four cut in front of Josh. Josh felt an urge to push Rick back, but he noticed a teacher was walking toward them. He was glad that the teacher intervened. What would you do if you saw this happening at your school?

This disrespectful behavior is an example of bullying. Bullying is *a type of violence in which one person uses threats, taunts, or violence to intimidate another again and again.* Bullies may tease their victims or try to keep them out of a group. They may attack them physically. Three out of four students have been bullied at one time or another.

What *are* Bullying Behaviors?

Bullies often taunt people who are shy or stand out in some way. Male bullies often use threats of physical violence.

Female bullies often use verbal put-downs that hurt other people's feelings. Different kinds of bullying include:

- **physical bullying**—hitting, kicking, pinching, spitting, tripping/pushing, taking personal belongings, or making mean or rude hand gestures.

Three out of **four** students have been *bullied* at one time or another.

- **verbal bullying**—teasing, labeling or *name-calling,* taunting, or making threats to physically harm.
- **psychological bullying**— intimidation or *purposely frightening another person through threatening words, looks, or body language,* spreading rumors, isolating a person, or threatening to use force, embarrassing in public.

Where Bullying Occurs

Bullying can happen almost anywhere during or after school hours. It can also occur on the school playground or bus, while going to or from school, in your neighborhood, or on the Internet.

What *is* Harassment?

Any behavior that is directed toward another person because of race, nationality, skin color, gender, age, disability, and/or religion becomes **harassment** or the *ongoing conduct that offends another person by criticizing his or her race, color, religion, physical disability, or gender.*

When harassment becomes violent, it might be a **hate crime.** A hate crime is *committed against another person because she or she is a member of a certain social group.* Harassment, though, is defined by Federal civil rights law. This law refers to harassment that is severe, persistent, or creates a hostile environment. It protects against harassment based on a person's:

- race
- nationality
- skin color
- gender
- age
- religion

Harassment that involves behavior or remarks of a sexual nature is called **sexual harassment.** It is *uninvited and unwelcome sexual conduct directed at another person.* Obscene or inappropriate e-mails, text messages, or voice mails with a sexual meaning can also be sexual harassment. This behavior is illegal.

Conduct related to harassment is **gender discrimination.** It occurs by *singling out or excluding a person based on gender.*

How Can I Respond *to* Harassment?

Our differences are what make us interesting. Making a joke about someone else because of that person's race, gender, ethnic identity, religion, or a

The facts about bullying are sometimes misunderstood. *Predict who is bullied more often—boys or girls.*

physical disability is harassment. Harassment is a crime. If you are a target of harassment, you can:

- Tell the person to stop. Say that if it continues, you will report the harassment.
- Be assertive. Speak firmly, looking the person in the eye.
- Tell your parents or other guardians. Ask for advice on handling the harassment.
- Report it to an adult. Harassment is illegal and charges can be filed against the person who is harassing you.

>>> Reading Check

IDENTIFY *Federal law protects against harassment based on what protected classes?*

Why Do Teens Get Bullied?

The reasons teens get bullied have little to do with the teen who is being bullied. A bully will target another teen because he or she is trying to fill an unmet need. Some teens may bully others to feel good about him- or herself. Being different in any way is one reason why a teen is bullied. It is common during the teen years to want to fit in with a group. However, as you become an adult, you will begin to value your individuality more.

Our differences are what make us interesting. Some people, though, are uncomfortable with differences. They may choose to become bullies and target teens who are different. Other reasons that teens may be targeted by bullies include those considered to be:

- different: being overweight or underweight, being uninterested in sports or athletics, wearing glasses or different clothing, being new to a school, or not having popular items.
- weak or unable to defend themselves.
- annoying or provoking.
- depressed, anxious, or insecure with low self-esteem.
- less popular than others and having few friends.
- unable to get along well with others.

Why Do Teens Become Bullies?

Teens who bully use their "power" to hurt people. The bully's power does not always mean he or she is bigger or stronger. The bully might be popular or smart—or the bully may know a secret about the person being bullied. Bullying is not a healthy behavior. Teens may become bullies because they feel that bullying behavior will help them

- fit in with a group.
- feel superior.
- avoid being bullied themselves.

Other times, a teen may become a bully because of behaviors that he or she learned from parents or others. In this situation, a teen may not believe that he or she is being a bully. He or she may feel that bullying behavior is okay because of a

- lack of tolerance of others who are different.
- lack of parental supervision.

Bullied teens may not be aware that bullies actually have low self-esteem. They pick on others to feel better or more important. Bullying others may make the teen feel superior. Also, a bully almost always needs an audience that supports his or her actions.

Many bullies have been bullied by other teens. So, they might bully as a way to be part of a group or to keep from being bullied themselves. However, this means that the negative cycle of bullying repeats itself unless the cycle is broken.

>>> **Reading Check**

EXPLAIN *What is one main reason that bullies hurt others?*

Bullies are not always confident and may have low self-esteem. *Describe the negative cycle of bullying.*

Robert A Pears/Photodisc/Getty Images

WHAT ARE THE EFFECTS OF BULLYING?

MAIN IDEA Anyone involved with bullying is affected in negative ways.

Everyone involved with bullying is affected—the bullies, those being bullied, and the people who watch the bullying. Bullying can contribute to many problems, including negative mental health, substance use, and suicide.

Teens who are bullied can experience negative physical and mental/emotional health. Teens who are bullied need to find someone to talk to about the bullying. Teens who are bullied are more likely to:

- feel fear, helplessness, depression, and loneliness.
- have low self-esteem.
- miss school or skip school.
- drop out of school.
- have various health problems.
- have trouble sleeping.
- inflict self-harm.

Bullies also experience effects and consequences for their bullying behavior. Many times, the bully may be seeking acceptance by bullying others.

Even though the bully is the aggressor, he or she may also experience mental/emotional and social health problems.

Bullies are more likely to:

- have low self-esteem.
- drop out of school.
- have problems with violence.
- have problems with substance abuse.
- have problems with criminal behavior.

It may seem that the teens who witness bullying are not affected by it. Unfortunately, even a teen who witnesses bullying, but does not participate will be affected by bullying. Teens who witness bullying when it happens can experience:

- increased use of tobacco, alcohol, or other drugs.
- increased mental health problems, including depression and anxiety.
- missing or skipping school.

> **Reading Check**
>
> **EXPLAIN** *What are some negative health effects of bullying?* ■

>>> **After You Read**

1. **VOCABULARY** Define the term *bullying*. Use it in an original sentence.
2. **IDENTIFY** Name the forms of bullying.
3. **RECALL** What are some forms of harassment?

>>> **Thinking Critically**

4. **APPLY** Your cousin writes to tell you about a "really funny kid" who just came to his school. He explains that this new person gets a laugh by knocking other students' books out of their hands. How would you explain to your cousin that this action is inappropriate behavior?

>>> **Applying Health Skills**

5. **ACCESSING INFORMATION** Harassment is considered a hate crime in 46 of the 50 states. Find out what the laws are in your community regarding harassment. Make a poster explaining the penalties for this behavior.

 Review

 Audio

Bullying affects everyone. *Describe the effects of bullying experienced by teens who witness the bullying.*

L. Mouton/PhotoAlto

Cyberbullying

> **BIG IDEA** Cyberbullying is a growing problem that causes harm and humiliation.

Before You Read

QUICK WRITE Write a poem or short story about a cyberbully. Give your poem or story a positive ending.

▶ Video

As You Read

STUDY ORGANIZER Make the study organizer on page 41 to record the information presented in Lesson 2.

Vocabulary

› cyberbullying

🔊 Audio

🔤 Bilingual Glossary

HOW IS TECHNOLOGY USED TO BULLY?

> **MAIN IDEA** Cyberbullying is more difficult to avoid than face-to-face bullying.

Cyberbullying is *the electronic posting of mean-spirited messages about a person, often done anonymously.* Technology includes devices and equipment such as cell phones, computers, and tablets. Cyberbullies use technology to harass people, threaten them, or spread rumors. Examples of the communication tools that cyberbullies use to send mean messages or spread embarrassing rumors, photos, videos, or fake profiles include:

- social media sites.
- text messages.
- e-mails.
- instant messages.
- chat rooms.
- websites.
- online gaming sites.

This type of bullying allows one person to bully another without ever seeing him or her in person. The person being bullied may not even be able to identify the cyberbully.

Because of this lack of face-to-face contact, the bully might not realize how much his or her actions hurt the other person.

Cyberbullies use **technology** to **harass** people, **threaten** them, or **spread rumors**.

Cyberbullying *vs.* Bullying

Both types of bullying target one person with the intention to harm or humiliate him or her. However, differences exist between cyberbullying and bullying:

- Cyberbullying can be anonymous and can be difficult to trace.
- Cyberbullying can reach a wider audience very quickly.
- Cyberbullying can happen at any time.

- Inappropriate or harassing messages, texts, and pictures are extremely difficult to delete after they have been sent or posted online.

These differences can make cyberbullying more difficult to avoid than face-to-face bullying. Teens who are cyberbullied have a harder time getting away from the behavior. In addition, teens who are cyberbullied may often be bullied in person as well.

Effects of Cyberbullying

Cell phones and computers themselves are not the cause of cyberbullying.

You can use social media sites for positive activities like connecting with friends and family, getting help with school work, and for entertainment. Unfortunately, these communication tools are also used to hurt other people.

Cell phones and *computers* themselves are **not the cause** of **cyberbullying.**

With more adolescents and teens using technology, the opportunities for cyberbullying have increased.

Whether bullying is done in person or through technology, it has negative effects on a person's physical, mental/emotional, and social health. Teens who are cyberbullied are more likely to:

- use alcohol and drugs.
- skip school.
- experience in-person bullying.
- be unwilling to attend school.
- receive poor grades.
- have lower self-esteem.
- have more health problems.

>>> **Reading Check**

LIST *What are the effects on a teen who is being cyberbullied?*

WHAT ARE SOME TYPES OF CYBERBULLYING?

MAIN IDEA Cyberbullies use several types of technology to attack another person.

Today, many people have access to technology whether it's at school, home, or through community resources, such as your local library. Many teens also have a cell phone that they use to keep in touch with family and friends. Having access to these tools has many benefits. Using computers and cell phones, however, can also make you vulnerable to cyberbullies.

Teens spend much of their social lives online, and so cyberbullying is more of a threat. *List other technologies that might be used for cyberbullying.*

The use of technology in everyday life has provided bullies with a number of new ways to attack another person. A cyberbully can use a computer to post false information on social media sites, in blogs, e-mails, and instant messages. Text messages can also be used to cyberbully.

As the use of technology increases, the ways that cyberbullies attack others will increase, too. Rather than avoiding technology use, think about what you can do to prevent cyberbullies from targeting you.

How Can I Prevent Cyberbullying?

The best way to avoid becoming the victim of a cyberbully is to do what you can to prevent it from occurring. Avoid including personal information about yourself in text messages, e-mail, or social media sites.

Another important rule to remember is that any photo that you post online will remain online forever. Even if you delete a photo, a person with good computer skills can retrieve the image. This includes photos that are sent via e-mail, posted to a social media site, or sent via text.

In some cases, cyberbullying begins as a result of a photo or message that one teen sends to another.

> You can avoid being a target of cyberbullying and also help others to protect themselves. *Evaluate whether you should respond immediately to a hateful text message from a cyberbully.*

Sexting, or the sending of explicit e-mails and photos, is always risky. It's also against the law if the person in the photo is under 18 years old. Any message or picture you send to another person is no longer in your control. The person receiving your message or picture can post it online or share it with others without your consent.

How Can I Stop Cyberbullying?

When cyberbullying happens, keep all evidence of it. Write down the dates, times, and descriptions of incidents. Save and print screenshots, e-mails, text messages, etc.

- Do not respond to or forward cyberbullying messages. Block the person who is cyberbullying. Visit the web site's help page to learn how to block users.

Stop Cyberbullying

Do Keep a record and evidence of attacks.	**Don't** Respond to the cyberbully.
Do Tell an adult if you receive harassing messages.	**Don't** Forward messages or images sent by a cyberbully.
Do Block messages from the cyberbully, if possible.	**Don't** Share or post personal information with strangers or people you do not know well.
Do Report the incident to your social media site, Internet provider, cell phone service, school, and/or local law enforcement agency.	**Don't** Visit websites that are unsafe.
Do Keep your passwords safe and do not share them with anyone except your parent(s).	**Don't** Post any text or images online that could hurt or embarrass you or those you know.

REVIEW

⟩⟩⟩ After You Read

1. **VOCABULARY** Define the term *cyberbullying*.
2. **LIST** Name the communication tools used by cyberbullies.
3. **EXPLAIN** What are three negative effects of cyberbullying on the victim?

⟩⟩⟩ Thinking Critically

4. **APPLY** Find Internet ads, or television commercials designed to stop bullying. How are the ads effective? How might the ads be more effective?

⟩⟩⟩ Applying Health Skills

5. **COMMUNICATION** A friend of yours has received humiliating text messages. What advice would you give her on handling this cyberbullying? Write a "To Do" list of strategies for your friend.
6. **DECISION-MAKING** A friend of yours has been receiving hurtful text messages. You know who is sending the messages. You want to be a good friend. You think about confronting the bully but worry that the bully will target you. Use the steps in the decision-making process to decide what to do.

 Review

 Audio

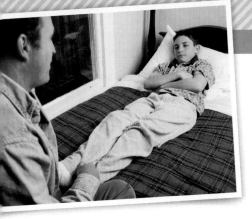

Strategies *to* Stop Bullying

BIG IDEA Every person can take steps to stop bullying behavior.

Before You Read

QUICK WRITE What steps do you take to keep yourself safe from bullying? Write a short paragraph about these strategies.

▶ Video

As You Read

STUDY ORGANIZER Make the study organizer on page 41 to record the information presented in Lesson 3.

Vocabulary

› bullying behavior

🔊 Audio

🅰🅱🅲 Bilingual Glossary

Myth vs. Fact

Myth: With more people using computers, cell phones, and wireless Internet, cyberbullying is on the rise.

Fact: Traditional forms of bullying are still more common than cyberbullying. Bullied people being hit, shoved, kicked, gossiped about, intimidated, or excluded.

HOW SHOULD I STOP A BULLY?

MAIN IDEA You can stop bullying now and in the future by using strategies.

Have you ever heard someone say, "What's the matter—can't you take a joke? You're just too sensitive." Comments like these might be directed at people who are targets of bullying. These remarks can make the bullied person feel as though he or she has no right to be sensitive. In some cases, the person who is bullied may feel that he or she deserves to be bullied.

No one deserves to be **bullied**.

On-the-Spot Strategies

No one deserves to be bullied. If you are a target, here are some ways to stop the bullying when it is happening:

- **Tell the bully to stop.** Look at the person and speak in a firm, positive voice with your head up. Say that if the behavior continues, you will report the bullying.

- **Try humor.** This works best if joking is easy for you. Respond to the bully by agreeing with him or her in a humorous way. It could catch the bully off guard.

- **Walk away and stay away.** Do this if speaking up seems too difficult or unsafe.

- **Avoid physical violence.** Try to walk away and get help if you feel physically threatened. If violence does occur, protect yourself but do not escalate the violence.

- **Find an adult.** If the bullying is taking place at school, tell a teacher or a school official immediately.

⟩⟩⟩ Reading Check

LIST *What are three ways to handle bullying on the spot?*

Do's

- Do keep control of yourself.
- Do stay calm and speak softly.
- Do walk away if necessary.
- Do apologize if necessary.
- Do try to turn the other person's attention somewhere else.
- Do use your sense of humor.
- Do give the other person a way out.
- Do try to understand how the other person thinks or feels.
- Do tell an adult.

Don'ts

- Don't let your emotions get the better of you.
- Don't let the other person force you into a fight.
- Don't try to get even.
- Don't tease.
- Don't be hostile, rude, or sarcastic.
- Don't threaten or insult the person.

Putting these tips to use can reduce your chances of being bullied. *Explain how you think these tips can help you avoid being bullied.*

>>> After You Read

1. **DEFINE** Define the term *bullying behavior.*
2. **LIST** Name two ways to stop bullying behavior.
3. **IDENTIFY** How might a bully try to correct his or her behavior?

Strategies *for* the Future

There are also several ways to avoid being bullied in the future:

- **Talk to an adult you trust.** A family member, teacher, or other adult can help. Telling someone can help you feel less alone. They can also help you make a plan to stop the bullying.
- **Avoid places where you know bullies target other students.** Stairwells, hallways, courtyards without supervision, and playground areas can be risky locations.
- **Stay with a group or find a safe place to go.** Bullies are less likely to target a student who is with his or her friends.

Stop Bullying Behavior

At times, a teen may not realize that his or her actions or words may actually hurt feelings. If you are someone who likes to joke with your friends, watch how the person responds to your jokes. If he or she seems hurt, stop the behavior.

Sometimes, a bully may not intend to hurt the feelings of another person. Some teens may need help recognizing **bullying behavior,** or *actions or words that are designed to hurt another person.*

If you have been called a bully or you think you might have bullied another person, follow these steps:

- Stop and think before you say or do something that could hurt someone.
- Talk to an adult you trust. Describe what upsets you about the other person.
- Remember that everyone is different, and that our differences make us interesting and unique.
- If you think you have bullied someone in the past, apologize to that person.

>>> Reading Check

IDENTIFY *What are some ways to avoid bullying?* ■

>>> Thinking Critically

4. **ANALYZE** Shayna is being teased repeatedly by Dejon. His remarks bother her. She doesn't know what to do. What advice do you have for Shayna?

>>> Applying Health Skills

5. **COMMUNICATION SKILLS** Your new classmate, Seth, is having trouble with a student who is bullying and teasing him. Seth feels uncomfortable facing the bully. What strategies would you offer Seth to help him deal with this problem? Explain why.

⟳ Review

 Audio

Promoting Safe Schools

BIG IDEA Students, teachers, and parents can promote schools that are safe from bullying.

Before You Read

QUICK WRITE Write a short paragraph about ways to stay safe from bullying in school.

▶ Video

As You Read

STUDY ORGANIZER Make the study organizer on page 41 to record the information presented in Lesson 4.

Vocabulary

› zero tolerance policy

◀» Audio

ⒶⒷⒸ Bilingual Glossary

Character Check

Caring for Others If someone you know has been bullied, you can demonstrate caring by showing concern and empathy for that person. Listen if the person wants to talk. Help him or her know when to seek help from a parent or other trusted adult. *Describe some other ways you could show the person you care.*

HOW CAN TEENS PROMOTE SAFE SCHOOLS?

MAIN IDEA By recognizing the signs of bullying, students can take a stand against it.

Keeping schools safe takes effort by students, as well as parents, teachers, and school officials. You can help by being aware of bullying and recognizing the signs of bullying. Then, if you are confronted by a bully or witness bullying, you can take a stand against it.

What Are *the* Warning Signs?

Bullying and harassment are not always obvious. Many teens who are bullies or are being bullied do not ask for help. Those being bullied may try to hide the problem from friends. They may be afraid or embarrassed to talk about it. However, many warning signs can indicate someone is being affected by bullying—either being bullied or bullying others. Recognizing these warning signs is an important first step for taking action against bullying.

It is important to talk with students who show the signs of being bullied. It is also important to talk to those who show signs of bullying others. These warning signs can also point to other issues or problems, such as depression or substance abuse. Talking to the person can help identify the cause of the problem.

Many teens who are **bullies** or are **bullied** do not ask for help.

Look for changes in behavior. Not all teens who are bullied show warning signs. However, certain signs may mean someone is experiencing a bullying problem. If you know someone in distress or danger, talk to a trusted adult right away. Likewise, students may be bullying others if they demonstrate several warning signs that you can learn to recognize.

Take *a* Stand Against Bullying

If you see someone else being bullied you may not know what to do to stop it. Using the following strategies can help the person who is being bullied.

- Tell the bully to leave the person alone.
- Offer an escape to the person being bullied by saying a teacher needs to see him or her.
- Avoid using violence and insults.
- Tell an adult.
- Tell the person who is bullied, "I'm here for you."
- Ask the person being bullied what you can do to help.
- Spend time with the person being bullied.

Warning signs can help identify teens who are being bullied or who may be bullies themselves. *List three signs of a bullying problem.*

Warning Signs of Bullying Behavior

Signs of Being Bullied	Signs of a Bully
Unexplained injuries	Getting into physical or verbal fights
Lost or destroyed clothing, books, electronics, or jewelry	Having friends who bully others
Frequent headaches or stomach aches, feeling sick or faking illness	Increased aggressive behavior
Changes in eating habits, skipping meals or binge eating. Coming home from school hungry because the student did not eat lunch.	Sent to the principal's office or to detention frequently
Difficulty sleeping or having frequent nightmares	Unexplained extra money or new belongings
Declining grades, loss of interest in schoolwork, or not wanting to go to school	Blaming others for his or her problems
Sudden loss of friends or avoiding social situations	Not accepting responsibility for his or her actions
Feelings of helplessness or decreased self esteem	Competitiveness and worry about his or her reputation or popularity
Self-destructive behaviors, such as running away from home, harming him- or herself, or talking about suicide	

Health SKILLS ACTIVITY

Conflict Resolution

Stand Up to *Bullying*

While walking to class, Molly sees a large group of students gathered in the hallway. Molly sees that two students, Tracey and Sarah are involved in an argument. Tracey is teasing Sarah about her outfit and calling her names. Sarah tries to walk away, but Tracey starts to push her against her locker. Sarah is very upset and needs help.

What Would You Do? Write a dialogue that shows how Molly can help Sarah escape this situation.

WHEN SHOULD I REPORT BULLYING?

MAIN IDEA At times, the best option for dealing with bullying is reporting the behavior to an adult.

Many schools are developing a zero tolerance policy, *a policy that makes no exceptions for anybody for any reason,* to bullying. In some cases, the policy may extend to bullying and cyberbullying that takes place off of school property. This type of policy provides students who feel helpless and isolated a way to stop the bullying.

Any teen who is bullied, or who has a friend who is being bullied, should tell a parent or teacher about the bullying. If necessary, tell more than one adult about the bullying. Stopping the bullying quickly can prevent it from becoming worse. If the bullying becomes violent, it should be reported immediately to a parent, teacher, or the police.

You should **tell a parent** or **teacher** if you or a friend is *being bullied.*

All bullying is wrong. If you see another teen being bullied, support that teen. Avoid teens who tend to bully others. Talk to your school administrators about starting an anti-bullying campaign at your school. Help educate other students about cyberbullying by talking about treating others with respect on social sites or the Internet.

>>> Reading Check

DEFINE *What does zero tolerance policy mean?* ■

Teachers who promote tolerance among teens can go a long way toward preventing conflict and bullying at school. *Identify a benefit of tolerance for teens.*

From Martin Barraud/Digital Vision/Getty Images

>>> After You Read

1. **DEFINE** Define the term *zero tolerance policy.*
2. **IDENTIFY** Who can help prevent bullying in schools?
3. **EXPLAIN** What are three warning signs of being a bully?

>>> Thinking Critically

4. **EVALUATE** Find out if your school has a program to deal with preventing bullying. If so, how might students become aware of the program? If not, do research to find a program that might help your school.

>>> Applying Health Skills

5. **APPLYING INFORMATION** You want your parent or guardian to learn more about bullying and how he or she can help prevent it. What would you explain to him or her? Write down some basic information on what parents can do to prevent bullying in schools.

🔄 Review

🔊 Audio

Hands-On HEALTH ACTIVITY

Be Part *of* the Solution

WHAT YOU WILL NEED

* blue construction paper (**Note:** Blue ribbon is the color used to support or create an awareness associated with prevention of bullying and child abuse.)
* scissors
* white Paper 8 ½ x 11
* markers
* glue

Everyone involved in bullying can be affected- the bullies, those being bullied and the people who watch the bullying. In this activity YOU get to make a positive difference by "Stopping the Hate" and promoting and advocating for a school that is safe from bullying.

WHAT YOU WILL DO

1. Take a white sheet of paper and carefully cut it into four equal squares with a scissors.

2. Review lesson one and from the information found in this lesson write a powerful statement on one square of white paper that will advocate and empower others to be part of the solution that ends bullying and harassment. Do the same for lesson two, three and four.

3. Using blue construction paper, trace your hand four times and cut out four handprints. On the fingers of each hand print write: "Be Part of the Solution"

4. Glue one square of paper with your empowering statement written on it to the middle of your handprint.

WRAPPING IT UP

Place the blue "Be Part of the Solution" handprints in your school at the beginning of the week. At the end of one week, write a reflection and identify how your "Be Part of the Solution" project advocated and influenced yourself and/or others to create a school safe from bullying. Discuss other activisms you can create to prevent bullying, harassment and cyberbullying in your school and community.

©Steve Skjold/Alamy

READING REVIEW

FOLDABLES and Other Study Aids

Take out the Foldable® that you created for Lesson 1 and any graphic organizers that you created for Lessons 2-4. Find a partner and quiz each other using these study aids.

LESSON 1 Bullying and Harassment

BIG IDEA Anyone can experience bullying and harassment, but there are effective ways to stop both.

* Most students have been bullied at one time or another.
* Anyone involved with bullying is affected in negative ways.

LESSON 2 Cyberbullying

BIG IDEA Cyberbullying is a growing problem among teens that causes harm and humiliation.

* Cyberbullying is more difficult to avoid than face-to-face bullying.
* Cyberbullies use several types of technology to attack another person.

LESSON 3 Strategies to Stop Bullying

BIG IDEA Every person can take steps to stop bullying behavior.

* You can stop bullying now and in the future by using strategies.
* By recognizing warning signs, you can help someone who is being bullied.

LESSON 4 Promoting Safe Schools

BIG IDEA Students, teachers, and parents, can promote schools that are safe from bullying.

* Students, teachers, and parents can all take a stand and help prevent bullying in schools.
* At times, the best option for dealing with a bullying is reporting the behavior to an adult.

 Review

 Web Quest

ASSESSMENT

Reviewing Vocabulary *and* Main Ideas

› bullying
› intimidation
› harassment
› cyberbullying
› labeling
› sexual harassment

» On a sheet of paper, write the numbers 1-6. After each number, write the term from the list that best completes each sentence.

LESSON 1 Bullying and Harassment

1. Purposely frightening another person through threatening words, looks, or body language is called _____.

2. _____ is a type of violence in which one person uses threats, taunts, or violence to intimidate another again and again.

3. Ongoing conduct that offends another person by criticizing his or her race, color, religion, physical disability, or gender is known as _____.

4. _____ is also referred to as name-calling.

5. Uninvited and unwelcome sexual conduct directed at another person is known as _____.

LESSON 2 Cyberbullying

6. Electronic posting of mean-spirited messages about a person, often done anonymously, is called _____.

» On a sheet of paper, write the numbers 7-12. Write True or False for each statement below. If the statement is false, change the underlined word or phrase to make it true.

LESSON 3 Strategies to Stop Bullying

7. <u>Bullying behavior</u> is actions or words that are designed to hurt another person.

8. Using <u>humor</u> can be a strategy to stop bullying when it is happening.

9. Bullies are <u>more</u> likely to target a student who is with his or her friends.

LESSON 4 Promoting Safe Schools

10. A policy that makes no exceptions for anybody for any reason is called a <u>zero tolerance</u> policy.

11. <u>Some</u> bullying is wrong.

12. Any teen who is bullied, or who has a friend who is being bullied, <u>should tell</u> a parent or teacher about the bullying.

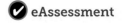 eAssessment

>> Using complete sentences, answer the following questions on a sheet of paper.

☁ *Thinking* **Critically**

13. **SYNTHESIZE** Zoey recently moved from a different part of the country. She speaks with an accent that is different than that of the students in her new school. Kathy, a girl in her class, imitates Zoey's accent, teasing her whenever she speaks. Kathy's teasing really bothers Zoey. What should Zoey do?

14. **EVALUATE** When Seth walks away from a fight, he hears the bully call him "chicken." What should Seth do? Explain.

⬤ *Write* **About It**

15. **NARRATIVE WRITING** Write a fictional story about a bullying incident. Describe the traits of the bully and the form of bullying that occurred.

16. **EXPOSITORY WRITING** Write a paragraph describing how a zero tolerance policy might stop bullying.

Ⓐ Ⓑ Ⓒ Ⓓ STANDARDIZED TEST PRACTICE

Reading
Read the passage below and then answer the questions that follow.

Bullying comes in many shapes and forms. A person might call you names or threaten you with physical violence. A person might tease you or try to keep you from a group. Bullies may even physically attack you. In recent years, technology has also given teens a new way to bully others. They might send a nasty message in an e-mail or through a website. In addition, they might post disrespectful messages about a person or post embarrassing videos.

If you're being bullied, try to ignore the person and walk away, if possible. Try to remain calm, even if the bully tries to prevent you from leaving. Be forceful and stand up for yourself, but try not to let the confrontation turn physical. It is important to report the incident to a person in authority, such as a teacher, counselor, or other trusted adult.

1. What does *confrontation* mean in this sentence from the passage?
   Be forceful and stand up for yourself, but try not to let the confrontation turn physical.
   A. conflict
   B. agreement
   C. compromise
   D. discussion

2. Which of the following best describes the purpose of the second paragraph?
   A. To explain reasons why people bully others.
   B. To describe how being bullying makes a person feel
   C. To suggest ways to deal with bullying
   D. To give reasons bullies should be tolerated

CHAPTER 1

Foldables®

Make this Foldable® to record what you learn about the six traits of good character in Lesson 1.

1 Begin with a plain sheet of notebook paper. Fold it in half so its long edges meet.

3 Open your Foldable® and cut six tabs along one edge of the paper.

2 Fold the paper into six smaller sections.

Define key terms and record facts about the six traits of good character.

Study Organizers

Use the following study organizers to record the information presented in Lessons 2–5.

Lesson 2:
Key Word Cluster

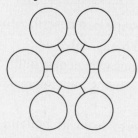

Lesson 3:
Two-Column Chart

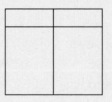

Lesson 4:
Bulls-eye

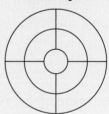

Lesson 5:
Three-Column chart

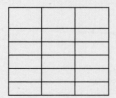

CHAPTER 2

Foldables®

Make this Foldable® to record what you learn about bullying, cyberbullying, harassment, and strategies to stop bullying in Lesson 1.

1 Begin with a sheet of notebook paper. Fold it along the long axis. Leave a ½" tab along the side.

3 Turn the paper vertically and label the tabs bullying, cyberbullying, harassment, and strategies to stop bullying.

2 Unfold and cut the top layer along the three fold lines. This makes four tabs.

Define key terms and record facts about bullying, cyberbullying, harassment, and strategies to stop bullying.

Study Organizers

Use the following study organizers to record the information presented in Lessons 2–4.

Lesson 2:
Venn Diagram

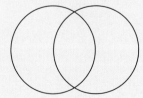

Lesson 3:
K-W-L Chart

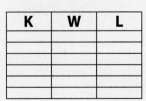

K	W	L

Lesson 4:
Key Word Cluster

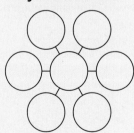

Glossary/Glosario

English

Español

Abstinence (AB stuh nuhns) The conscious, active choice not to participate in high-risk behaviors.

Accountability A willingness to answer for your actions and decisions.

Advocacy Taking action in support of a cause.

Attitude (AT ih tood) Feelings and beliefs.

abstinencia Opción activa y conciente de no participar en comportamientos de alto riesgo.

responsabilidad Voluntad de responder de tus acciones y decisiones.

promoción Actuar en apoyo de una causa.

actitud Sentimientos y creencias.

Bullying A type of violence in which one person uses threats, taunts, or violence to intimidate another again and again.

Bullying behavior actions or words that are designed to hurt another person.

intimidar Tipo de violencia en la cual una persona usa amenazas, burlas, o actos violentos para intimidar a otra persona una y otra vez.

El comportamiento de intimidación cualquier comportamiento que se dirige a otra persona que use los comentarios hirientes, amenazas o violencia.

Character The way a person thinks, feels, and acts.

Clique A group of friends who hang out together and act in similar ways.

Communication The exchange of information through the use of words or actions.

Conflict resolution A life skill that involves solving a disagreement in a way that satisfies both sides.

Constructive criticism Using a positive message to make a suggestion.

Cultural background The beliefs, customs, and traditions of a specific group of people.

Culture the collected beliefs, customs, and behaviors of a group

Cumulative (KYOO myuh luh tiv) risk When one risk factor adds to another to increase danger.

Cyberbullying the electronic posting of mean-spirited messages about a person often done anonymously.

carácter Manera en que piensas, sientes y actúas.

camarilla Grupo de amigos que salen juntos y que se comportan de manera similar.

comunicación Intercambio de información a través del uso de palabras y acciones.

resolución de un conflicto Habilidad que implica el hecho de resolver un desacuerdo satisfaciendo a los dos lados.

La crítica constructiva Spanish Definition: Con un mensaje positive a hacer una sugerencia.

base cultural Creencias, costumbres y tradiciones de un grupo específico de personas.

cultura Colección de creencias, costumbres y comportamientos de un grupo.

riesgo acumulativo Cuando un factor riesgoso se suma a otro e incrementa el peligro.

El acoso cibernético la publicación electronica de la media mensajes animados sobre una persona hace a menudo anónimamente.

English

Español

Decision making The process of making a choice or solving a problem.

tomar decisiones Proceso de hacer una selección o de resolver un problema.

Empathy Identifying with and sharing another person's feelings.

empatía Identificar y compartir sentimientos de otra persona.

Environment (en VY ruhn muhnt) All the living and nonliving things around you.

medio Todas las cosas vivas y no vivas que te rodean.

Fraud A calculated effort to trick or fool others.

fraude Esfuerzo calculado para engañar a otros.

Goal setting The process of working toward something you want to accomplish.

establecer metas Proceso de esforzarte para lograr algo que quieres.

Harassment (huh RAS muhnt) Ongoing conduct that offends another person by criticizing his or her race, color, religion, physical disability, or gender.

acoso Conducta frecuente que ofende a otra persona con críticas sobre su raza, color, religión, incapacidad física, o sexo.

Health The combination of physical, mental/emotional, and social well-being.

salud Combinación de bienestar físico, mental/emocional y social.

Health care any services provided to individuals or communities that promote, maintain, or restore health

cuidado medico Cualquier servicio proporcionado a individuos o comunidades que promueve, mantiene y les hace recobrar la salud.

Health care system All the medical care available to a nation's people, the way they receive the care, and the way the care is paid for.

sistema de cuidado de la salud Servicios médicos disponibles para a la gente de una nación y las formas en las cuales estos son pagados.

Health fraud The selling of products or services to prevent diseases or cure health problems which have not been scientifically proven safe or effective for such purposes.

fraude médico Venta de productos o servicios para prevenir enfermedades o curar problemas de salud que no han sido aprobados científicamente o hechos efectivos para ese uso.

Health insurance A plan in which a person pays a set fee to an insurance company in return for the company's agreement to pay some or all medical expenses when needed.

seguro médico Plan en el que una persona paga una cantidad fija a una compañía de seguros que acuerda cubrir parte o la totalidad de los gastos médicos.

Health maintenance organization (HMO) A health insurance plan that contracts with selected physicians and specialists to provide medical services.

organización para el mantenimiento de la salud Plan de seguro de salud que contrata a ciertos médicos y especialistas para dar servicios médicos.

Health skills skills that help you become and stay healthy

habilidades de salud Habilidades que ayudan a ser y mantenerte saludable.

Heredity (huh RED I tee) The passing of traits from parents to their biological children.

herencia Transferencia de características de los padres biológicos a sus hijos.

Hospice care Care provided to the terminally ill that focuses on comfort, not cure.

asistencia para enfermos Asistencia para personas con enfermedades incurables que apunta a brindar comodidad, no a la cura.

Glossary/Glosario

English

I

"I" message A statement that presents a situation from the speaker's personal viewpoint.

Integrity Being true to your ethical values.

Intimidation Purposely frightening another person through threatening words, looks, or body language.

L

Labeling Name-calling.

Lifestyle factors Behaviors and habits that help determine a person's level of health.

Long-term goal A goal that you plan to reach over an extended period of time.

Loyal faithful

M

Managed care A health insurance plan that saves money by encouraging patients and providers to select lest costly forms of care.

Media Various methods for communicating information.

Mind-body connection How your emotions affect your physical and overall health and how your overall health affects your emotions.

P

Peers People close to you in age who are a lot like you.

Prejudice (PREH juh dis) A negative and unjustly formed opinion.

Prevention Taking steps to avoid something.

Preventive care Steps taken to keep disease or injury from happening or getting worse.

Primary care provider Health care professional who provides checkups and general care.

Español

mensaje yo Declaración que presenta una situación desde el punto de vista personal del orador.

integridad Ser fiel a tus valores éticos.

intimidación Asustar a otra persona a propósito con palabras amenazantes, miradas o lenguaje corporal.

marcar Dar nombre.

factores del estilo de vida Conductas y hábitos que ayudan a determinar el nivel de salud de una persona.

meta a largo plazo Objetivo que planeas alcanzar en un largo periodo de tiempo.

leal fiel

cuidado controlado Plan de seguro médico que ahorra dinero al limitar la selección de doctores de las personas.

medios de difusión Diversos métodos de comunicar información.

conexión de la mente con el cuerpo Forma en la cual tus emociones afectan tu salud física y general, y como tu salud general afecta tus emociones.

compañeros Personas de tu grupo de edad que se parecen a ti de muchas maneras.

prejuicio Opinión formada negativa e injustamente.

prevención Tomar pasos para evitar algo.

cuidado preventivo Medidas que se toman para evitar que ocurran enfermedades o daños o que empeoren.

profesional médico principal Profesional de la salud que proporciona exámenes médicos y cuidado general.

English

R

Refusal skills Strategies that help you say no effectively.

Reliable Trustworthy and dependable.

Risk The chance that something harmful may happen to your health and wellness.

Risk behavior An action or behavior that might cause injury or harm to you or others.

Role model A person who inspires you to think or act a certain way.

S

Sexual harassment Uninvited and unwelcome sexual conduct directed at another person.

Specialist (SPEH shuh list) Health care professional trained to treat a special category of patients or specific health problems.

Stress The body's response to real or imagined dangers or other life events.

T

Tolerance (TAHL er ence) The ability to accept other people as they are.

V

Values The beliefs that guide the way a person lives.

W

Wellness A state of well-being or balanced health over a long period of time.

Z

Zero tolerance policy A policy that makes no exceptions for anybody for any reason.

Español

habilidades de rechazo Estrategias que ayudan a decir no efectivamente.

confiable Confiable y seguro.

riesgo Posibilidad de que algo dañino pueda ocurrir en tu salud y bienestar.

conducta arriesgada Acto o conducta que puede causarte daño o perjudicarte a ti o a otros.

modelo ejemplo Persona que inspira a otras a que se comporten o piensen de cierta manera.

acoso sexual Conducta sexual no solicitada y fuera de lugar dirigida a otra persona.

especialista Profesional del cuidado de la salud que está capacitado para tratar una categoría especial de pacientes o un problema de salud específico.

estrés Reacción del cuerpo hacia peligros reales o imaginarios u otros eventos en la vida.

tolerancia Habilidad de aceptar a otras personas de la forma que son.

valores Creencias que guían la forma en la cual vive una persona.

bienestar Mantener una salud balanceada por un largo período de tiempo.

normativa de tolerancia Normativa en que no hay excepciones para nadie por ninguna razón.

Index

Index

Understanding, 11

Values, in decision making, xxii
Verbal bullying, 24
Verbal communication, xx
Volunteering, 15

Walking, F4F-5

Walking programs, F4F-2
Warm-ups, F4F-1
Websites, reliable information from, xviii
Wellness
    defined, ix
    health vs., ix
    and mind-body connection, x
Wellness Scale, x
Words, showing character through, 13
Working together, to build good character, 6

Zero tolerance policies, 35